'B' COMPANY

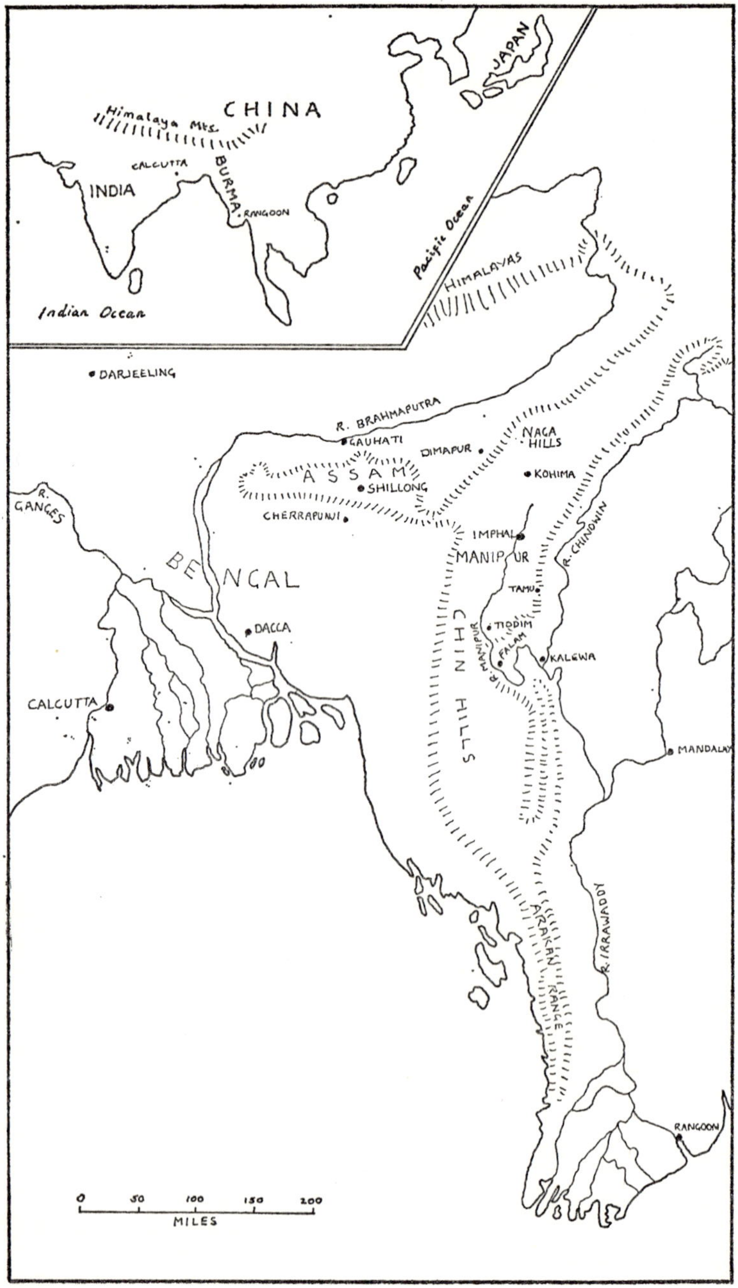

CHINA
Himalaya Mts.
JAPAN
INDIA
CALCUTTA
BURMA
RANGOON
Pacific Ocean
Indian Ocean
HIMALAYAS
DARJEELING
R. BRAHMAPUTRA
GAUHATI
DIMAPUR
NAGA HILLS
ASSAM
SHILLONG
KOHIMA
R. GANGES
CHERRAPUNJI
IMPHAL
MANIPUR
R. CHINDWIN
BENGAL
TAMU
DACCA
TIDDIM
CHIN HILLS
R. MANIPUR
FALAM
KALEWA
CALCUTTA
MANDALAY
ARAKAN RANGE
R. IRRAWADDY
RANGOON
0 50 100 150 200
MILES

RAYMOND COOPER

'B' COMPANY
9th Battalion
THE BORDER REGIMENT
48 Brigade
17 Indian (Light) Division
IV Corps
14th Army
South East Asia Command

*One man's war in Burma 1942-1944
recalled in hospital in 1945*

LONDON : DENNIS DOBSON

Copyright © 1978 by Raymond Cooper
All rights reserved

*First published in Great Britain in 1978
by Dobson Books Ltd., 80 Kensington Church Street, London W8 4BZ*

*Printed in Great Britain by
Bristol Typesetting Co. Ltd,
Barton Manor, St Philips
Bristol*

ISBN 0 234 72063 8

To
Arthur Behrend
who was a writer

FOREWORD by

Admiral of the Fleet the Earl Mountbatten of Burma,
KG, PC, GCB, OM, GCSI, GCIE, GCVO, DSO, FRS

Many books have been written about the Burma Campaign. I, myself, was instructed by the Combined British and U.S. Chiefs of Staff to write a report about the operations of the one and a third million Allied Soldiers, Sailors and Airmen in South-East Asia who turned continuous defeats into total victory against the Japanese. Indeed when I visited the Burmese Defence Services Academy at Maymyo on 14th February 1972 I found my report had been translated into Burmese and was their principal military text book. But this account was written on the Supreme Commander's level and could give no insight into the day-to-day life of the smallest cohesive units, such as Infantry Companies of just over 100 men.

This splendid book fills this gap admirably. It gives the human, and sometimes inhuman, side of the continuous fight against an implacable, fanatical foe. I found it fascinating and absorbing for the author takes us through the entire life span of the 9th Battalion of the Border Regiment 'B' Company over the three years he commanded it. When he left his command, after being severely wounded, his Company had suffered such terrible casualties in battle that the survivors were merged with 'D' Company as a different entity.

The book will bring back many vivid memories to those who fought under the frightful conditions in Burma, and also satisfaction that we won through. From the day I set up my command I visited and spoke to as many units as possible on all three widely separate fronts. I told them that the Japanese were not 'born jungle fighters' and that we could outfight them in the jungle provided we never let them force us to retreat. The withdrawal of 17 Division, described in this book, was intentional to fight our pitched battle against the massive Japanese attacks on the Imphal Plain, but it was a hazardous and brave withdrawal.

But what I hope most is that the younger generation will read this book and discuss what their fathers, and by now even their grandfathers, went through in the war, their fortitude and courage to fight against the unprovoked aggressors. And to learn how futile and crazy war really is.

Mountbatten of Burma
A.F.

PREFACE

'B' Company was formed at West Hartlepool in Co. Durham with the nucleus of a Battalion made up mostly of the 24/25 year old call up, together with a few regular soldiers home from service in India with 2nd Battalion. The majority of recruits came from the true Border counties of Cumberland and Westmorland, but there was always a sprinkling of Tynesiders plus the invaluable Cockney, while later a strongish contingent of reinforcements joined from Liverpool and Yorkshire.

I, at Sedbergh in January 1939, by-passed the many worries of the future officer by being commissioned in the School O.T.C. and by doing what corresponded to my O.C.T.U. training at Aldershot before being posted to the 9th Battalion The Border Regiment in 1940.

The following account was written in hospital during February 1945 without any maps, diaries, or personal records, and it had been impossible to check the exact details of distances, mileages, etc.

When many years later a chance reading led the manuscript to the printer rather than the incinerator, the illustrations and diagrams of Sgt. Hutchinson and Pte. Towner were made available by courtesy of Lt. Col. J. Petty, M.B.E., M.C. and the Trustees of the King's Own Border Regimental Museum, Carlisle. I am most grateful to them for their ready help.

Also to the fact that such a simple, personal, account should now be honoured with a Foreword by Lord Louis

Mountbatten which revives once more the effect his appointment as Supreme Allied Commander South East Asia Land Forces had at the time.

It gave a touch of imagination and hope not just to those who knew something of his brilliant father and his own brave record but to all the men in the field who had already sensed that given the tools our forgotten army could beat the enemy and who now knew that we would be seen to share a common war with Europe and with the Americans too.

When soon after the appointment was announced the 'Supremo' himself visited, not just Corps Headquarters 200 miles behind us, but our jungly group at 9000 ft in the Chin Hills, he made one demand: a box on which to stand so that all available troops could gather round and look him in the eye.

Not only Rangoon but Tokio itself seemed suddenly on that damp winter afternoon at last within our reach.

CONTENTS

Chapter		Page
I	ENGLAND	15
II	AT SEA	25
III	INDIA	29
IV	SHILLONG	41
V	THE ROAD	49
VI	THE CHIN HILLS	57
VII	PATROLLING	70
VIII	M.S. 22	91
IX	OPERATION NECKLACE	98
X	DOWN THE ROAD	109
XI	SIEGE OF IMPHAL	117
XII	THE ROAD AGAIN	129
XIII	UP THE CHIMNEY	145
	EPILOGUE	148

SOUTH EAST ASIA COMMAND

(Other land, sea and air forces)

14th ARMY

XV Corps — Reserve troops

IV CORPS

20th Division — 23rd Division

17th DIVISION

Artillery — Engineers

INFANTRY

16th Brigade — 63rd Brigade

48th BRIGADE

1/7th Gurkha Rifles — 2/5th Gurkha Rifles

9th BATTALION, THE BORDER REGIMENT

HQ Coy. — 'A' Coy. — 'C' Coy. — 'D' Coy.

'B' COMPANY

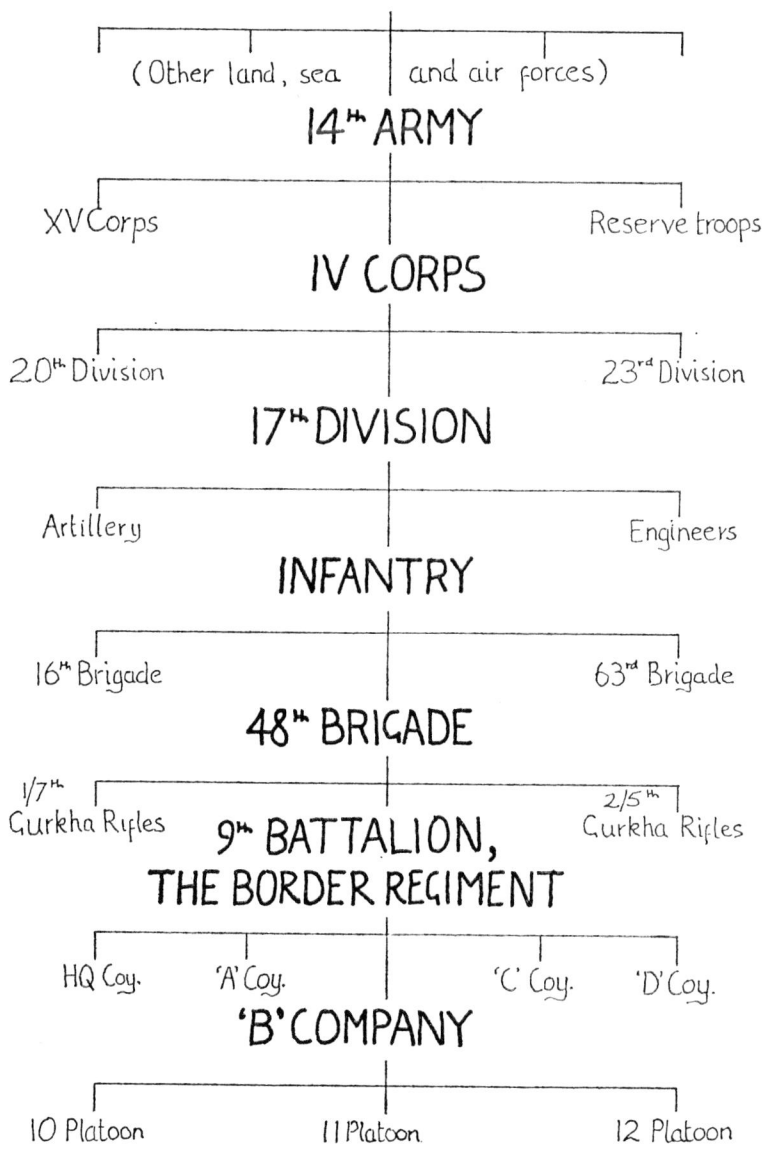

10 Platoon — 11 Platoon — 12 Platoon

Although the structure of South East Asia Command was constantly changing, this diagram shows 'B' Company's position in the Command in 1942/3

I

ENGLAND

'B' Company first shook itself out into the minor entities of Platoons and Sections at Cockermouth, in Cumberland, in the late summer of 1940. There, with its officers billeted in the Globe Hotel and its troops in the workhouse, it learnt to give fire orders on to sheep on Lowther Fell, or to point its weapons at targets among the Lakeland rocks. Three years later those lessons were to be tested among the towering ranges on India's eastern frontier, with the yellow-faced Jap moving in the very same sights that then had framed the black-faced Herdwick.

Battalion H.Q. was ten miles away in Workington and, until I joined them in December as Intelligence Officer, my chief memories as a subaltern of the Company with which I was fated to spend all but three months of my soldiering career is of route marches lit by the brisk sunshine and glorious colours of that lovely autumn. None of the men would ever confess to having walked anywhere for pleasure, yet few, I suspect, will ever forget those weekly fifteen or twenty miles set against the glory of Bassenthwaite's autumn trees, or against the brick-red bracken lighting the way over Whinlatter Pass.

We travelled in what we thought those days was full equipment. We carried rifles or pistols, but Bren guns were assumed to come along with other awkward articles like ammunition and anti-tank rifles in Platoon trucks. Packs were worn, but the empty mess tins and water bottles they contained did not yet foreshadow the days when every man would carry four days' rations on his back and when a refill for a water bottle was going to be as difficult to come by as a spare bandolier.

Our two enormous sandwiches each for lunch were carried then in the 15 cwt truck which represented all our Company transport, and the biggest thrill of the morning was to be in the leading Platoon when they first sighted the smoke rising in the sunny, frosty air from the Colour Sergeant's Soya stove and knew that the 'brew' was not far off, and that soon they would be resting and drinking a pint of that rich, hot, brown liquid which Army cooks can always produce out of ordinary tea-leaves.

C.Q.M.S. Knight was a Cockney, and one of those people it was difficult not to call by his nickname of 'Rocky'. This breach of Army etiquette also applied to 'Taffy' Young, the C.S.M. Not that either was in the least easy-going when on duty for both were regular soldiers, and it was from them and from Gavin Elliot, the Adjutant, that I learnt to deal not only with that side of the Army which depends on paper for its existence but also with the Mess and Dress traditions which every good regiment owns.

Moreover it was the experience of men like these upon which one depended for knowledge, for if it is true that most of the art of soldiering is common sense it is also common sense that in all its years of endurance the Army will usually have hit upon the best way of doing a thing, and it is a mere waste of time for everyone who dons a uniform for the first time in war to pretend he knows better.

But where I did have skirmishes with Authority was when the military institutions would not adjust themselves to the new type of material that had come under their rule in wartime. Many a time I was respectfully rebuked by C.S.M. Young for allowing men to speak to me directly, because the Army required soldiers to ask pompously for a private interview with an Officer or to state their case whilst standing to attention in Company office under the vigilant eye of the C.S.M. This system may often be necessary with men to whom soldiering is a permanency, but to the beginner who comes from fells or dales sympathy can be stifled at birth, or the townsman may feel the beginning of an antagonism with authority.

Another line on which I differed was in the treatment of junior N.C.O.s, the individual training of whom I classed second only to general weapon training in its vital importance. In peace-time the man is trained and waiting to take his place as an N.C.O., and is at once capable of earning his stripes without further help except an occasional talk on Regimental customs by the R.S.M. In war one selects a likely man from the raw material and then shows him his job.

When we came to do our fighting we fought in the murk of the jungle, and it was 'B' Company's good fortune in those early days in Cumberland to possess the material from which to build.

This is by no means a treatise in any form on how soldiers should be trained, and if I have digressed from the story of 'B' Company's memories, or should do so again, it is because that story must always to me be bound up in my own feelings and in life as I saw it at the time.

Finally, and while I am so much off the track, let me say that I know of few people who can so directly affect the lives of those near to him as a Company Commander. A Battalion Commander has fierce responsibilities of life and death, and can make an unbelievable difference to the general standard of his men. But he cannot personally know his command in the way a Company Commander must know his Company of 120 or so lives. It is the Colonel who will ask for a Tiger Patrol of a Corporal and a Private, but it is the Company Commander who chooses Corporal Anderson and Private Baker, two men whose lives, wives, and fancies for the future he knows intimately.

To return, I took a spell away from the Company in December 1940 to become Intelligence Officer and Assistant Adjutant at Battalion H.Q. My Intelligence work consisted in finding and training a Section of a Sergeant and six men in the pleasant jobs of making maps, drawing panorama, and making battle deductions, but I also learnt the workings of the Battalion as a unit. From the C.O. himself I learnt the discipline of orderly room, and I also learnt to respect at first hand the tenet in military life that the man who assumes the position of Colonel is all-powerful, whatever his character, breed, or brain. From the Adjutant, whose 'stand-in' I was, I learnt to view the Battalion as a unit shaping itself for the purpose of becoming fit to fight, yet treading also within its training the well-trodden paths of discipline and smartness.

Thus the winter of 1940 passed, with an interval over Christmas for an excellent sniping course at Bisley where, even if we were not all made into marksmen, we were at least taught how to teach shooting—a surprisingly neglected art in a wartime army. We spent long hours on the ranges shooting from 100^x to 1000^x or crawling over the heath disguised as tree-stumps or pieces of Bisley Woods. A party further enlivened by a Christmas Eve spent mostly in persuading several Czechs on the course that, even if Santa Claus was their fellow-countryman, they didn't have to climb down the Commandant's chimney to wish him a Happy Christmas.

In February 1941 the Battalion moved across to the Northumberland coast, and I took over 'B' Company for what was to be an uninterrupted spell of over three years. The Adjutant had been on leave until the day I took over, and as a result I arrived at a wind-swept tent in a field on the sand flats opposite Holy Island at about 8 o'clock at night. There was by way of being an anti-invasion signal scheme on at the time, and it seemed much more important that the Company should be killing off the thousands of theoretical Germans who were supposed, having evaded shipwreck on the Farne Islands, to have landed on our piece of beach than to go into all the fuss of taking over an Infantry Company. So the outgoing Company Commander said: 'You'd better sign a few bits of bumph, old boy; there's some money in that black box, the C.S.M. has the Company roll, and I think you'll find everyone has a weapon of some sort. Excuse me if I go off and pack.'

And I signed 'the few bits of bumph', and dragged the horror-stricken C.S.M. to the beaches to look at my defences. Later, at a Company Commanders' course at Northallerton, I was told my take-over should have lasted a week!

All was well, however. There was some money in the black box, and everyone produced a Bren gun or rifle when I had my first arms inspection. In fact those nine Bren guns—five of which were not new when we started—were used for all weapon training and all practice shooting, and were the identical nine that eventually went into action against the Japanese. They lasted in fact too well, because the minor complaints which afflicted them in battle allowed several daring yellow men to live a good deal longer than they deserved.

I now had the thrill of training my own Company and of learning to assess the individual personalities which comprised it. Not only that. We now held a front line position in Britain's defence and, even allowing for the gap across the North Sea, we might be said to be standing face to face with the German conquerors of Europe. Not perhaps much of a front line compared with south-east England, but it didn't stop the feeling that something depended on us at last, and the excitement was always fanned by a succession of knowledgeable lecturers who all worked up to the climax that there was bound to be an invasion of Britain soon, the likeliest place for the Germans to choose was Northumberland, the most vulnerable part of Northumberland was just where we were stationed, the most certain time was as soon as moon and tides were together, and the moon and tides would join forces the following night!

Spurred on by these arguments we toiled through February, March, and April in the snow and icy winds of northeast England. Officers and men alike spent all the hours of daylight trying to make their numbed fingers weave a barbed-wire fence from Bamburgh to Berwick-on-Tweed or digging weapon-pits in sand as volatile as quicksilver. Company Commanders were occasionally important enough to get away from the beaches for a conference but the inevitable result for the troops was that three rolls of Dannaert had to be put up instead of two, or a new set of weapon-pits scraped out of the sand to satisfy the theories of our latest visitor from Division.

Night work was worst. Outside every military unit, or sub-unit, some unfortunate had to spend the night 'on stag' staring into the cold night and feeling he had never really appreciated his night's sleep in peacetime. And there were of course innumerable night ops.—mostly designed to train the Company to keep control of direction in the dark, but sometimes more ambitious as when we embarked in Holy Island fishing boats and practised 'invasion' by moonlight on the undaunted mainland a mile away.

Apart from all the guards—on our ninety-mile stretch of coast we had innumerable little H.Q.s, or isolated gun sites—the threat sometimes held over our heads was not of invasion in force, but of little squads of Germans equipped with powerful wireless sets and sneaking in in rubber boats which popped out of the submarines which infested our shores. To combat this peril we had to patrol the shore from what was called 'Hot water' in the evening until 'Good visibility' after dawn, code words which covered the time during which other watchers of the coast such as the lighthouse-keepers on Holy Island could not see far enough to spot any visitors arriving from the continent.

It was all right on paper, like so many other schemes arranged on maps or in offices, but when one had to wear enough clothes to keep out the north-easter, and came to trudge those bleak beaches clogged by sand, sometimes by snow, it merely became a question of 'doing one's best'. I found in 'B' Company the men had been set impossible jobs to do at night, merely because the officers had not attempted them themselves. In fact during my first week a 2,000-ton ship was wrecked during the night on our bit of beach, yet patrols out looking for 'little rubber boats' came home in the morning with 'nothing to report'!

I knew well enough my patrols couldn't cover all the ground as often as ordered, and I just altered Brigade orders and still feel unrepentant about having done so. It sounds easy enough to say to higher authority that its orders are impossible, but this is seldom done. Provided a Company Commander can achieve results there is no disloyalty to the inflexible rule that an order must be obeyed. Isn't it by cutting short a lot of contradictions and countermandings, and by trying to ensure that orders which do reach troops have reason behind them, that implicit obedience in the final test of battle is obtained?

Well, the weather gradually improved. Defences took shape, and we were able to get on with the job of sorting out our N.C.O.s and training for battles to come. By the nature of our job on the coast, Battalion H.Q. was a long way off and seemed unduly glad to leave Company training to Company Commanders. Certain directives were issued to us and the hints they contained always appeared in print in Company Training Programmes, but provided one kept an eye open for the infrequent appearance of the Commanding Officer (for whom one could always put on a special show) one could indulge one's fancy, one's originality, or one's idleness to one's heart's content. We even had a Company Commander, an ex-ranker of the 1914-1918 war, whose theory was, 'I don't believe in all this training; it will be different in the trenches'! But it was different again in the jungle, and he didn't last to see the effect on his Company of his constant kit inspections and unadorned route marches.

Meanwhile we had to rely on our own young ideas and we were still comparatively unhelped by courses which were dull affairs then compared with the virile things they became later.

My particular training fancy was for Field Firing, that is to say shooting our Company weapons not from the comfort of a range but as in the discomfort of battle and at targets as varied and realistic as possible. Over the fields and sand dunes of Northumberland we could indulge in this as long as ammunition would permit without doing more damage than waking the Home Guard or splashing a passing ship or bouncing a ricochet off the *Flying Scotsman* at a certain point where the L.N.E.R. line comes rather close to the coast.

I had a Sergeant Devlin with me at the time, a man who revelled in making bangs and in taking risks of all kinds, and we used to spend the days firing small arms and grenades at, over, or round our troops, and the evenings trying by many methods not in the text-book to detonate grenades unexploded during the day's adventures. These proceedings were often enlivened by the loose mines which floated in daily from the North Sea.

We moved across the northern part of Northumberland quite a bit in 1941. Cheswick, Elwick, Goswick, Lowick, Fenwick, Alnwick, and various other 'wicks housed us in tent or billet at one time and another, but wherever we were the week always contained a great deal of walking. A weekly route march combined with map-reading was a regular feature, and marching was always the main feature when we did Brigade or Divisional exercises with the Northumberland Division. I remember it particularly while 'B' Company was stationed at Alnmouth and the rest of the Battalion was billeted inland, and much nearer the moors where our schemes took place. 'B' Company had that extra seven miles to do before crossing the Start Point, and at night we would file back down the same old road to the sea, Sections on either side, Company Headquarters making its usual run of jokes in the middle, everyone, blistered and unblistered alike, wondering if for once we were going to get in before closing time.

The big advantage of war as played with umpires and blank cartridges was that one got very tired, and one spent two, three, or even four nights in cold and uncomfortable positions, and then there would be Rest, and sometimes Leave.

On one memorable scheme my Company H.Q. was on an Alnwick pavement for three days. While we sent out patrols and dealt with an enemy which enjoyed the distinction of soft caps instead of steel helmets, a pub on one corner and a cinema on another and a canteen in between carried on their normal functions within a few yards of us. In the end even the Brigadier succumbed voluntarily to a gas attack, and as he expired in the Great Hall of Alnwick Castle he conferred on me the freedom of Northumberland and with it the right to command such motley force as had survived from drastic umpiring. He then exchanged his deathbed for a more comfortable billet while we sallied forth into the night.

* * *

During all this time my Company had acquired, if nothing else, a reputation for fitness. We won the most ambitious of the Battalion training schemes, which consisted of a cross-country march finishing up with a Field Firing exercise in which time, tactics, and shooting scored points. And No. 12 Platoon won a Grand Divisional March across the Cheviot Hills carrying all its arms and ammunition, and arriving twenty-one minutes in front of the General who was to welcome us and forty minutes ahead of our runners-up, a platoon of the Green Howards.

We were living that week under canvas on the land of Mr Rae near Belford, and I think it was the eggs he produced for breakfast together with the barrel that awaited the victors' return which spurred them on. Indeed the farmers who found their pastures smothered in barbed-wire or ravaged by anti-tank ditches or through whose hedges we crawled were consistently kind. And so was everyone else. I well remember the day when the Company finished an exercise at dawn near a small cottage, and I went over to investigate the disappearance of half of them. They were being fed on tea and cake by the old lady who lived there. She would take no money, and she said she had saved her rations for just such an occasion.

So the busy days passed. A month on the Tyne would make a chapter, the hospitality of Newbiggin-on-Sea over the New Year was only matched by the friendliness of the miners in the small town of Cambois where we were twice billeted. Our second exit was a little blurred by the transport that should have fetched the Company at noon not arriving till half past two. These happened to be the opening hours of the Miners' Club in which Company H.Q. and two platoons had been billeted.

When we weren't training today we were thinking about training tomorrow, when we weren't putting up new defences we were pulling down old ones. Until eventually and after a month of the dullest of all jobs—guarding the aerodrome at Acklington—we found ourselves in April 1942 on the right side of the Tweed, three miles from the nearest pub, and therefore ready for that train which was to take us to Glasgow and overseas.

The Border Regiment badge

II

AT SEA

Two Generals and one Brigadier had told us we were going to India, we had all had two embarkation leaves apiece, we had been issued with topees, tropical shorts and labels galore, yet not until the sugary verses of 'There'll always be an England' floated across Glasgow Docks and we found ourselves with three gunner regiments, a complete General Hospital, and sundry military odds and ends on board S.S. *Orcades* and moving down the Clyde did most of us fully realize the implications.

Very few of the Battalion had seen active service, and in the years we had waited at home the first flush of our volunteer excitement had rather dulled our expectations of anything ever happening. Now we were off. Something was bound to happen, and everyone leaned over the rails on deck, wondering after what experiences and in what company he would see home again. And I wondered how much fitter we were to serve then than when we first left our homes and jobs to join the Army. We had learnt to use our weapons and to keep ourselves smart and fit, we had learnt the camaraderie that comes from barrack-room and route march and from the football we played with other Battalions or with Hawick, Jedburgh and the Border clubs. No longer was any one of my sentries likely to startle the Brigadier with the remark, 'Halt! Advance one and recognize me.' But had we needed as much as two years of this kind of preparation?

* * *

The *Orcades* was a lovely Orient boat, and the officer accommodation in early 1942 was still very much on the lines of a peacetime cruise. We had two sittings for meals. But we had first-class cabins, lounges, a swimming pool, a concert hall, and a large promenade deck, which was used for parades by day and for walks with the General Hospital in the evening.

Conditions for the troops were far less pleasant. Tiers of hammocks were slung along the mess decks as thick as cells in a hive, queues formed halfway round the ship for meals, canteen, even for baths. Very few of the men had been to sea before though several had worked in the Barrow shipyards in peacetime and some had even helped to make the ship on which we now sailed.

There were plenty of things to occupy our minds while the easiest way of living this crowded new life was gradually being worked out. We proudly wrote On Active Service on our last letters home, and we felt as we handed them in without stamps that some notice was at last being taken of our war effort. We watched our convoy companions anchoring near us in the Clyde, we watched one Sunday evening the hills of Arran and then the rocks of Ulster fade into the twilight, we awoke with a thrill in the morning to find a convoy 'just like in the pictures' spaced out across the grey Atlantic. *Nelson* and *Rodney* pounded along off our port bow, and an aircraft carrier and our destroyer escort kept station away on the horizon.

It was roughish for the first five days, and this dulled interest in life for many, but under our new Commanding Officer, who had taken over just before we left England, the Battalion for the first time began to feel itself a single unit. We had the big open 'A' deck allotted to us once a day for P.T. and weapon training. Sometimes we had route marches with the Battalion band playing, a form of exercise the troops had not expected would follow them to sea. Much to the astonishment of the R.A. regiments, we even practised a form of deck parade-ground battle drill complete with flanking movements, supporting fire, and consolidation. There were lectures by officers from the other units on non-infantry subjects including Douglas Jardine on war in Australia; and there was always a dash to practise boat stations, to fill in any idle moment.

Three months went by before we finally docked at our destination, but the boredom we had all expected was missing. The Germans were battering their way towards Stalingrad and Alexandria, but we basked in the sea air and sunshine of the Atlantic and Indian Ocean with nothing more exciting than the frequent zig-zagging of the convoy to remind us that we were part of the war we had almost forgotten.

At Freetown, where the convoy put in for water, we first tested our topees and tasted our first spell of tropical heat. For fear of mosquitoes the troops were not allowed to sleep on deck while we were in harbour, and even the air coming through the blowers was as stifling as we imagined it to be inland in the thick forests which lay behind the red and green hills backing the water-front.

We didn't however go ashore until a month later when we said good-bye to the *Orcades* at Durban, and waited a fortnight in the transit camp at Clarewood. Our destination was still officially India, but a strong rumour started that we were to join the welcome to Rommel in Egypt. So, once again to the surprise of the gunners and other non-infantry inmates of our camp, we rushed about in a flurry of training, and thereby missed our white man's share of the famous South African hospitality.

Incomprehensibly to the Border Regiment at least it was, of course, very strictly a white man's share. Black Americans who arrived in the next convoy expecting equal treatment soon had to be confined to barracks when they assumed they could travel wherever there were seats on the train instead of crowding into the nigger hutch at the back.

However we did not have too bad a time. One of the accepted methods of training was to march to the bathing beach at Isipingo, and there dismiss the Company until it was time to return in the evening, and night or day made no difference to South Africans ready to take all and sundry for car drives, picnics, and parties the moment we were free. Some of us had too good a time, because when we embarked in the *Empire Trooper* six of my men sneaked ashore in the dark and we sailed without them. They were reinforcements from South Lancashire who had joined us just before leaving England.

There were few facilities for movement or amusement this voyage but we had old *Orcades* friends on board in the L.A.A. Regiment and the General Hospital, and the *Empire Trooper* was a friendly little ship, though her passengers swore she travelled sideways. The Egyptian rumour was soon scotched and we settled down for a month across the water to Bombay. After dinner at night my Second-in-Command and I, perhaps a little more sentimental than usual on Navy gin, would sit in the bows watching the sparkle of the phosphorescence in the water sliding by. The troops were humming their favourite songs, 'The White Cliffs of Dover' and 'Deep in the Heart of Texas', and if on occasions Maurice's slight hiccup marred the harmonies, well, who minded? We felt with Housman 'Shoulder the sky, my lad, and drink your ale,' and who knew when such company would cross the Indian Ocean again?

Raymond Cooper

June 1942
Isipingo, South Africa

R.A.C.,
Gavin Elliot,
Andrew Osborn-Smith

1942
Fort William,
Calcutta

standing:
Stan Blamire
J. W. Johnson
Arnold Schlund

seated:
R.A.C.
Maurice Allen

1943 Calcutta
Battalion
Rugby Team

Christmas Day 1942
Kulgachia, Bengal
Officers' guard mounting

left to right: Sgt. Carter, Maurice Allen, Mick Durkin, Sgt. Little, Arnold Schlund, Pte. James, Cpl. Whenray, R.A.C., Sgt. Leonard

The inspection by Mick Durkin and Pte. James

October 1943 Shillong, Assam 9th Battalion, The Border Regiment

October 1943 Shillong, Assam The officers of 9th Battalion, The Border Regiment

left to right standing:
Lt. Brodrick, Lt. Johnstone, Lt. Schlund, Lt. Blamire, Lt. Scott, Lt. Robinson, Lt. Petty, Lt. Johnson, Lt. Bibby, Capt. Simmons, Capt. Maconochie (I.A.MC), Lt. Girling, Lt. White, Lt. Revell

left to right sitting:
Capt. Thompson, Capt. Allen, Maj. Elliot, Maj. Spedding, Lt.-Col. Verbi, Maj. Travers, Maj. Cooper, Maj. Osborn-Smith, Capt. (QM) Brackpool

Himalayan leave

Brig. R.T. Cameron

R.A.C.

Privates
Rushforth,
Green and Wilcocks

January 1944 Vital Corner

left to right:
Schlund, Johnstone, R.A.C., Dukes,
C.S.M. Baynes

At War

Johnny Gurkha

Mike Hodgson, Reg Hunt

**Looking South
from Kennedy Peak**

**Kennedy Peak
Chapel exterior**

towards Fort
White and Falam

and interior

M.S.12

Company cooks

Mess at Vital Corner

'Dynamite' Dukes'
Padre Hazel,
Arnold Schlund

Vital Corner

Johnty bathing

Exit from the mess

Mike Hodgson

Coy. H.Q.

left to right:
Pte. Precious
C.S.M. Baynes
R.A.C.
Pte. Reed
Pte. Green
C.Q.M.S. Matheson
Pte. Dade
G.L. Paterson

Tiger Patrol to Pimpi
Pte. Hunter, Sgt. Larke, Johnty

Looking towards Hung Vum Mual and the Chindwins

Coy H.Q.

left to right:
Pte. Precious
C.S.M. Baynes
Cpl. Paterson
R.A.C.
Pte. Reed
Pte. Dade
Pte. Green
C.Q.M.S. Matheson

February 1944
Patrol to
Dollouang

.... with mule

Supremo: Admiral Lord Louis Mountbatten
  Commanders
Corps: Lt. Gen. Sir Geoffrey Scoones
Division: Maj. Gen. D. Tennant (Punch) Cowan
Brigade: Big. R.T. Cameron

SEAC Souvenir 1975

Battalion: Col Verbi
going on leave

Company: R.A.C.

Kennedy Peak
from the South

Battlefields

Hill 52
M.S. 22

Imphal

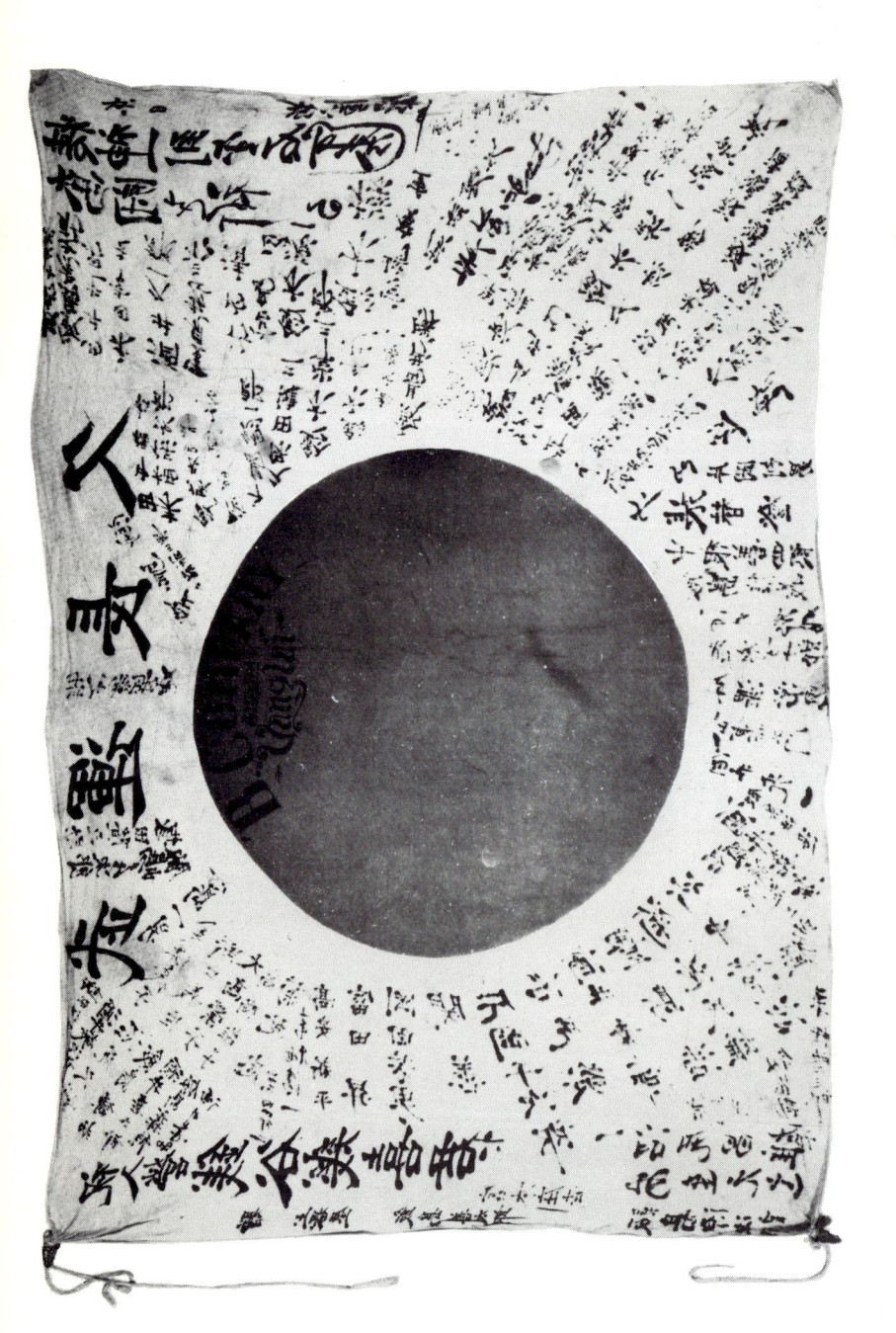

Japanese Flag captured by 'B' Company at Vanglai and presented to R.A.C.

III

INDIA

Everything always seemed to happen at week-ends, and it was a Saturday afternoon when the palms and palaces of Bombay showed up over the horizon. The burning question of our rôle in India was soon answered. To our consternation the Embarkation Officer announced we were due for Internal Security duties at Fort William in Calcutta.

Actually it was a pleasant enough assignation, but we were feeling somewhat restive after three months at sea and soldiers who had only seen India for half an hour were heard to protest indignantly they hadn't come all this way to act as policemen to a lot of natives. The news was much more galling to the regulars from the 2nd Battalion like the C.O. and Gavin Elliot who had recently left that very station in Calcutta to go to Europe to fight.

Meanwhile a farewell party with the General Hospital sisters (who were doing some rapid juggling for position on finding some of their stations were to coincide with batteries of the A.A. Regiment!), an illicit visit to the Taj Mahal Hotel next day for lunch with some friends off another ship, a final lecture on 'Care of arms in India', from the Second-in-Command, and we boarded the train for a five-day journey across the continent.

I don't think the troops were ever prepared to like India, about which they were one and all lamentably ignorant, and that particular train was the worst possible start. Crowded in twenties and thirties in smelly carriages with hard wooden seats, we ran hours—eventually days—late on our schedule, and travelled only through monotonous country of the Deccan. At every station we were screamed at by beggars or naked children for 'baksheesh', and there was little to remind our insular north-countryman of the land he loved and had left behind him.

There seemed to be two things chiefly at fault. The first was the narrowness of general education in Britain, which apart from its other faults did not seem to have imbued anyone with the desire to learn more than was immediately connected with the earning of his living. The other was the good old feeling of 'it's not like that in my back garden so it can't be right out here'. This sentiment may have fortified some outposts of Empire in the past, but it allows little hope of reaching an understanding with their present-day inhabitants.

My experience of India (this paragraph is bound to happen sooner or later, and I'll get it over while the train clatters its way across a continent over which so much ink has already been spilt by most of its visitors) was of an immense apathy which one sensed whenever one tried, in however good a heart, to discuss its problems. Nationalism was the root of it all. It was no good saying 'You have your freedom now in nearly all but name, and you admit you are not yet ready to take on defence, trade, justice, etc., without British help'. The answer, however hidden in verbiage, was 'Leave us alone and free to sort out the mess in our own way'.

The people who did not say this were either the silent few whose lives had always been wrapped up in British service or the vast majority of equally silent peasants who lived each in his own tiny area of an immense continent and who understood nothing of the complex military, religious, and political problem which so shook the outside world.

I, arriving like any other who had read anything of India's seemingly insoluble difficulties, found them just as insoluble as every sane writer is willing to confess. But I also found two things I had not been expecting, the enormous value of the types acting for Britain as District Commissioners or in any other responsible job such as the Forest Service, and the essential good looks of the people of India as a whole—not the beautiful features of the women one saw at race meetings and social functions or their florid and handsome husbands, but the fresh and often aristocratic faces of the boys who hired out bicycles or were employed as assistants by the fruit and other 'wallahs' infesting the towns. If looks mean breeding even the sweepers of India are descended from kings compared with the vicious run of humanity one sees in the bazaars and on the dockside of the Middle East and even in many European towns.

Largely because of all this I liked India, and I couldn't help regretting so little effort was being made to help thousands of officers and troops to understand the continent they were visiting for the first time. As it was, their first contacts were usually made with the scheming Bengali, and naturally enough all this added up to the generalization that 'the country stinks'.

* * *

So far as we were concerned a bad impression was made from the start. The Battalion had been less than a day in Fort William when the C.O. and the Company Commanders were ordered off on a tour of Calcutta. Riots were taking place, and one broke out on our path. We were ambushed in Harrison Street, and the police had to open some very indiscriminate fire to get us out.

Gandhi had been imprisoned again, and in the troubles which ensued we were called upon to supply guards and escorts of all kinds. These were in addition to the normal and innumerable static guard duties in Calcutta, and our troops found themselves travelling all over India from Delhi to Ceylon and even to the railheads of Assam. It was hard and thankless work, and often a Lance-Corporal and a couple of men were away on responsible jobs for weeks at a time with few provisions for their travel and with food difficult or very expensive to get.

Under these conditions it was extremely difficult to get on with Company training, and most of our time was spent on details of small military importance or in continuing to worship the ancient gods Blanco and Brasso and in polishing up our previous reputation as the Shiny 9th. This life soon palled, but even so Calcutta was a first-class station in which to learn army life in India under almost peacetime conditions. In Fort William itself we had our own church, cinema, swimming bath, squash courts, football, cricket, and hockey fields. On the Maidan outside was the Calcutta Rugby Club, the grounds of the famous Bengal Soccer Club, and a most lovely cricket field at Eden Gardens. Not much more difficult to get to were the Bengal Club, the Golf Club at Tollygunge, the Saturday Club, the Three Hundred Club, the Swimming Club, the several air-conditioned cinemas in Chowringhee.

It all sounds, and for a while it was, remarkably pleasant—for the officers. The troops just could not afford to go out more than once a week, and even then the European clubs were barred to them as strictly as to Indians.

Individual families were charming in their entertainment for the troops, and the Garrison Chaplain was able to organize occasional tea parties or visits to the Hoogli jute mills. But welfare as such in 1942 was completely unorganized. Even troops coming from the Burma fighting were getting into trouble with the Military Police for wearing the dirty clothes which were all they possessed.

Companionship, especially girls, was what the troops wanted most, but the few girls available were usually too haughty to make friends or too dusky to be selected. As in all cities women were freely available for money for those that wanted it that way, but here again the troops were the losers. The officer-sahib got soft lights and sweet music, and at least broken English for his rupees, but the soldier for his annas had to be content with some poor Hindu widow who for once had become an asset to her family and who probably carried with her the seeds of disease.

It was an ugly problem, and civil and military solutions supplied only the ostrich's answer. The Church said firmly that no problem existed, but few who preached that doctrine appreciated the difference between their own up-bringing and that of the men to whom they preached, and fewer still had been parted for four or five years from all hopes of family life.

Anyway it never became the major problem with us that it did with some Battalions, and as the civil disturbances quietened down we were able to spend more and more time in the country outside Calcutta training to fight an enemy we now knew was going to be the Jap.

Some good pamphlets were beginning to arrive, but Jungle Warfare was still very much in its experimental stages and 'Bungle Warfare' still seemed to most people a better description of our efforts.

We found a cleared area which consisted—like all the rest —of paddy fields and mud-made villages, and there, disturbed only occasionally by R.A.F. who used it for bombing practice, we could practise our field firing.

We developed, without much enthusiasm, the technique of marching through the flooded paddy fields up to our waists in water. The whole thing looking level enough from the top with just the long blades of rice growing through the water, but on more than one occasion a short-waisted soldier would walk innocently into some underground hole and his surprised neighbour would suddenly see nothing but the top of a steel helmet or the tip of a bayonet floating like some strange growth amid the rice.

This was not the least of our water troubles though. So many good lives had been lost in 1941 in the Salween and other bridgeless Burma rivers that improvised river crossings became the order of the day. A river, which to us meant a deep forty-yard-wide drainage ditch, was approached—usually with a bridge and several boats in sight in both directions—and the orders were to get across without using either.

The ubiquitous bamboo growing along the banks was generally assumed to be the answer, and many a strange craft varying from a couple of empty water bottles to a complete boat made of bamboo, groundsheets, and petrol cans set sail on the dirty waters of Bengal. One such containing three Bren guns, nine rifles, and sundry Tommy guns capsized in the deepest part, and for nearly two hours a Company Commander, his Sergeant-Major, and sundry Privates were to be seen diving naked under a tropical sun salving their precious cargo from among the mud and leeches of the river bottom.

Surprisingly few men could swim at this stage—nearly all learnt later—and those who could usually over-estimated their strength when weighed down with equipment and boots and weapons. I pulled out three men one day and two more later in the week as they sank helpless a few feet from land with their full packs and their clothes sodden with muddy water.

The last rescue was quite funny—for spectators. The C.O. had come to watch my Company practise a demonstration scheme we were laying on for Field-Marshal Wavell, then on a visit to Calcutta as Commander-in-Chief in India. The river crossing had gone quite well, and only my batman and I were left to get across. His name was Green and he was a superb batman and a very good friend to me for over three years, and I won't sing his praises beyond saying that my Army life was made at least twice as easy because of his good care and ever-present cheerfulness. But he would say 'Yes' to everything he thought I expected him to do, and if I had suggested it he would have cheerfully set off to fly to China or even to capture Mandalay single-handed. And so it happened now. To my horror I saw him swimming a steady breast stroke but gradually vanishing under the water.

The C.O. was watching and this time I determined to make a flashy rescue of it. I dived in and turned myself and Green on our backs in the approved style. Unfortunately I was to cross the river not dressed for life-saving, and as I turned over on my back my steel helmet filled with water and my chin strap slipped down to throttle my neck. I was soon in as bad a shape as Green, and every time I pushed him up for air I had to pull him down and heave myself up on him to get a breath for myself. In this jack-in-the-box fashion we eventually reached the shore, where we were helped out by the C.O.— who, somewhat misplacedly I thought, was roaring with laughter. And the joke was that from the moment I had reached Green I never pulled him under the water at all, and mine was the face which kept appearing every few seconds gasping for breath! To cap it all when Wavell did come the demonstration was changed to one on our assault course in Calcutta. After it was over, however, he insisted on meeting every man in my Company individually, so we felt it was not all for nothing.

As the turn of the year brought heat and hard grounds instead of our western winter we roamed further afield through the paddy fields and startled villages while learning to keep direction and control in a land without landmarks, and under the brilliant energy of the C.O. we evolved on our own tactics which were to be invaluable in the much more difficult country over which we would have to fight.

In the jungle, where surprise can so easily be effected, I was an enormous believer in battle drills of various kinds, something which would give instantaneously the best reaction to ambush, to sudden attack on a hidden bunker, or to the quick shaking out of a patrol into a defensive position. I 'discovered' none of this. It was all there in the pamphlets or developed in our talks during training, but like a lot of the Army's sound tactics too many people left them alone in the same way as A.C.I.s or King's Regulations as impractical things brought out only on courses or in the lecture rooms of O.C.T.U.s.

Some of this training was pleasant enough. I shall never forget the early, dewy mornings in the paddy fields in the one cool half-hour of the day, or lying out in those bright tropical nights when never a leaf was stirring yet the whole air purred with the ceaseless hum and crackle of countless insects. A lot of it was very exhausting as the days became hotter, and we seemed to be recording as many miles marched per week as ever we did in Northumberland. However all of it was very necessary to keep up the standard of a Battalion stationed in enervating surroundings like Calcutta, and it reminded us we were not always going to have fans to keep us cool, charpoys to sleep on, and 'charwallahs' to bring us tea and cakes at intervals between meals.

It was a relief, too, when 'B' Company was sent out on detachment to a place called Kulgachia to guard two vital railway bridges which carried the main lines to Bombay and Madras over the Damodar river. Here there was only rail communication and we were left to run our own show. To enable us to do so two native villages had been evacuated, one on either side of the river. Much to their amusement the troops lived in threes and fours in the mud-walled and thatch-roofed village houses, which were, however, remarkably clean. I was ensconced like the local rajah in the one brick bungalow in the centre.

Eleven Platoon lived on the opposite bank to the rest, and to meals they had to go round by the bridge—about a mile's walk—or cross in one of the native boats left in our charge. The crossing was only about 100 yards wide, but until they learnt a bit of watermanship it was a close race between the boaters and the walkers.

Christmas 1942 came while we were at Kulgachia, and the Battalion sent us more than our share of beer and birds and of everything else that makes it the one day in the Army year when militarism does not seem to predominate.

At least that was the way in 'B' Company, and each year we contrived to throw rank as nearly overboard as possible, and take a hundred per cent holiday. All except the inevitable guard. Even in the blazing Bengal sunshine Christmas still 'worked'. We got up late for breakfast, and in the absence of a padre we held our own service among the palm trees—though I disappointed the soldier who was heard to say 'He lectures us on something three hundred and sixty-four days of the year, and I suppose today he'll try a ruddy sermon'. After that we had sundry competitions in which the officers were summarily defeated at darts, deck-tennis, climbing coconut palms, and at anything else for which they entered, and we completed the morning with the officers' guard mounting ceremony. This was an annual performance at which we were inspected by one Private Durkin accompanied by the youngest soldier in the company as his Orderly Sergeant, and we took over all guard duties for a few hours so that no troops would miss their Christmas dinner. It was always an amusing session because we wore highly irregular clothing and we were armed with kukris, assegais, iron tubing and other irregular weapons, and Durkin had the best fund of native wit of any man in 'B' Company.

We then served the troops with the enormous dinner the cooks had spent the morning preparing and at which the C.O. by tradition came to pay his respects, and eventually we finished quenching our own appetites by about four o'clock in the afternoon.

Had we been at home most of the troops would have had friends to go to in the evening, but at Kulgachia with no white man in sight for miles around we had to arrange something else. So we held an impromptu regatta with our assorted river craft. Maurice Allen organized it, and I as chief judge was anchored in mid-stream on the roof of an enormous gondola, around which the lesser craft gyrated like corks in a whirlpool. Various events took place in quick succession, but the thing I remember best is the sight of the cooks, who had lunched extremely well, endeavouring to paddle a very round and temperamental boat across the stream. They entered for the first race, and they were still in roughly the same position an hour and a half later when the party finished. The highlight being when one of them announced languidly, 'I'm going ashore,' but as the boat turned round once more while he was making this announcement he stepped off on the wrong side in water up to his neck!

On Boxing Day what was intended to be a route march finished at an American Mission where the Sisters miraculously produced an enormous tea for nearly a hundred troops, and the rest of the week was spent parcelling up into ferry loads the enormous crowds of refugees who had fled after one small air raid on Calcutta. We then received an urgent message to return at once, and by dint of stopping a local train until we had all our stores on board and by fighting our way through the indescribable chaos of Howrah station at midnight in an air raid we reported the Company back to Fort William, to be greeted with, 'Oh, are you back, old boy? I expect there must be a scheme on.'

But there was no scheme on, and life for many weeks was personally enlivened only by a visit to the Jungle Warfare School at Sevoke in the jungles of northern Bihar. It was run by Major Robin Parry, M.C., of the 2/5 Royal Gurkha Rifles, and embodied all the ideas on jungle fighting learnt by 17 Division during its retreat through Burma and in later fighting with the Japanese in the Chin Hills.

It was excellent stuff. Not only were there demonstrations of all the intricacies of this new type of fighting, but one met officers and N.C.O.s straight from actual fighting units. The course finished with a three-day scheme which, in the country we covered and in the mock fighting we took part in, was a first-class test for the endurance and quickwittedness on which our lives were soon to depend.

Incidentally it was on that course I had almost my only view of the fearsome wild life which is supposed to infest all jungles. An American gunner acting as leading scout on a scheme with me took a hazardous snap shot at the flash of yellow as a tiger crossed our path; two elephants were drinking in a stream we patrolled one night looking for imaginary Japs; an N.C.O. with a Tommy gun bagged a king cobra and an enormous python on two consecutive days, and far more leeches appeared in the schemes of Sevoke than during our months of fighting in the 'official' jungles of Burma. The American who one night took off his blood-filled boot to find thirty-two leeches sucking at his foot and remarked wearily, 'I thought something was tickling,' showed a good sense of the proportion of our discomforts.

But in spite of the hours spent crawling through the jungle, in spite of the nights we leapt out of bed as gelignite slabs blew holes in our huts, in spite of the three days spent on six rashers of bacon and a packet of biscuits, in spite of the hours of learning to hack bamboo into everything from a canoe to a teapot, and the hours of soaking in the river Tista, even in spite of the booby traps we so constantly fell into, we learnt a lot from that course and we enjoyed it—or so we said when we were back among the fleshpots of Calcutta! And generally we lost no time in putting our troops through the paces we had just been made to tread ourselves.

But when I returned to the Battalion I found several things had happened to cast considerable gloom over its enthusiasm. Reinforcements were needed in the Arakan, and we were to supply thirty men from each Company—and they had to be our best—to join strange regiments at forty-eight hours' notice. Furthermore, General Irwin had stated that our particular branch of his Eastern Army was very low on the priority list and would not see action for many months, and—worst blow of all—our Commanding Officer had already left us on the next stage of promotion to his inevitable Brigade. Luckily I now got away for two weeks' trekking in the Himalayan foothills around Sikkim and Darjeeling, but that lovely leave cannot be called part of the story though 'B' Company doubtless gained from their Commander's improved temper.

Soon after my return the revolution of some tiny wheel within the complex machinery of G.H.Q. Delhi, set us off at last on the road to the war, for which we had trained for two years. The new C.O. had just agreed that we needed training pastures other than the well-trodden paddy fields of Bengal, and Green and I were sent off to investigate the jungles of Orissa. There we crashed the motor-bike on which we both rode, and after a night with the Forest Officer at Angul we returned to Fort William with seven stitches each in our right knee-caps only to find our quest and our stitches in vain. The Battalion had been ordered to join the Seventeenth (Light) Indian Division forthwith.

We had been praying for a move anywhere, but this was action with a vengeance! 17 Division had been in the long fighting retreat through Burma under General Alexander, and had ever since maintained at least part of its two Brigades in contact with the Japanese in the Chin Hills and Mytha Valley. We were to take the place of the British Battalion at present with them and we were to join the 2/5, 1/7, 1/3, 1/4, and 1/10 Gurkha Rifles—figures which we already knew by repute to stand for some of the finest fighting troops in India.

Our Arakan reinforcements were to return to us at once, everything we wanted (except those new Bren guns) was to be given to us, and we were to report to Shillong without delay.

IV

SHILLONG

Movement Control eventually started us off on our journey in the midst of the monsoon weather that made Calcutta feel like a permanent hothouse, and in spite of some well-planned delays organized by its Practical Jokes Department we gradually approached Shillong, 5,000 feet up in the Assam hills. The trip was in three parts, each an improvement on the last. In the train we were invariably abandoned by the engine during the hottest part of the day, and we fed on bully beef and hot tea while even the flies flew fewer sorties than usual in the heat and while the carriage roofs melted gradually away.

Life became cooler and more interesting when we transferred to a river steamer on the Brahmaputra. It was good enough to be sailing for even twenty-four hours on a river which had girdled the Himalayas, though we also had a night storm as exciting in its way as a tropical hurricane. During the day we had shooting competitions at everything floating past, from the wreckage of the storm to an occasional crocodile, in fact we steamed into the ferry port of Gauhati as noisily as *Showboat* firing a broadside.

The night we spent under canvas at Gauhati was the hottest I ever remember. But early next day we loaded in cars and on ramshackle buses and started climbing through the jungles and forests of the lower slopes towards the cooler tea gardens of Assam. En route we were welcomed by representatives from our new Brigade and by many little Gurkhas wearing the Black Cat sign of the 17th Division.

General Cowan had under his command in addition to the Gurkhas a Battalion of the West Yorks which was motorized in jeeps or carriers but destined—like the rest of us—to do most of its fighting on its feet, a Battalion of the Baluch Regiment to be used as mounted infantry, a Battalion of Frontier Force Rifles for protection of Divisional and Brigade H.Q.s, a Regiment of mule-borne 3.7 mm mountain guns, and a Regiment of 25-pounders.

For us the biggest change was the changing of all wheeled transport—except two jeeps per Company, one for ammunition and one for food—for mules. We had ten mules in each Company to carry ammunition. Apart from that, however, each Company Commander was allotted a 'charger', and every other item had to be carried in packs on our backs. The men took well to their new jobs as grooms and muleteers, and it wasn't long before our erstwhile drivers and motor mechanics were busy feeding and grooming their new charges.

Shillong was grand after the months in Calcutta. There were hills again and trees, clear-running rivers and friendly sunshine—and fresh air. Even the flies which had been with us since we landed in India seemed to have been shaken off, perhaps because they were deceived by the security regulations connected with the move, and we were to soldier with seasoned troops under a famous Brigadier and we felt at last that our hours of preparation were not going to be wasted.

Previously there had always been behind it all that faint shadow that we might in the end come to nothing, that we might get split up, or spend our time on some L. of C. job. In fact it had been like wondering if the last line of some sentimental poem you had been reading in *Punch* wasn't going to turn round and laugh at you.

Meanwhile all Company Commanders went to the 4th Corps School at Mawphlang some fifteen miles out from Shillong, and I myself stayed on for a few weeks afterwards to command a composite Demonstration Company. We also made a film of a Company in the attack and of other battle scenes for some war correspondent. Thanks to plenty of gelignite explosions and a few Gurkhas in Japanese uniforms to represent the deflated enemy it made quite a realistic show and saved him the trouble of going any nearer the front.

One of the best things on the course was meeting the officers from our fellow Gurkha Battalions and doing our patrols and river crossings and village clearing and sundry other schemes in the company of men who had come straight from action against the Japanese. For—in addition to another 4th Corps Division on the Tamu road—our fellow Brigade was still in contact with the enemy beyond Tiddim in the Chin Hills.

More and more now 'The Road' began to creep into our conversation. This was the famous highway built from railhead at Dimapur and running some three hundred miles through Kohima and Imphal to Tiddim, then on to the Chindwin at Kalewa. There were no towns on that road beyond Imphal, and milestones such as 82, 109, 126 became our landmarks just as Tobruk and Bardia and Benghazi were those of the 8th Army on its road to Tripoli.

But for still a few months yet 'The Road' to us was to remain as imaginative as the Highwayman's 'ribbon of moonlight over the purple moor' and so long as there was ammunition to play with and so long (sometimes longer) as there were soles on our boots we continued with the infantryman's eternal task of shooting and marching, marching and shooting.

Between Cherrapunji and Mawphlang we learnt the difficulties of using a one-inch map when marching across the grain of a country where the valleys were as deep and steepsided as the cracks in a dried mud flat. One night we were so lost that the only direction I could give to possible stragglers was to 'keep between the moon and that black hill on the right', yet the policy of entrusting all route-finding to the N.C.O.s of the leading Platoon paid rich dividends later when those same men were on long and lonely patrols, though it accounted for a number of unnecessary miles in those early training days.

At Happy Valley, the name of our camp outside Shillong, we toiled each week round our assault course. In its high jumps, long jumps, and balancing tricks it combined enough feats to qualify for Olympic Sports or an Olympia Circus, and the Company Commander who fell off the rope-bridge during a demonstration shall be nameless. But he can vouch for it that a hundred Japanese would have constituted a lesser obstacle.

At Barrapani we camped for a week while we paddled or swam across the lovely river at all hours of day and night, and we learnt to blaze trails and avoid making tracks, and all the other Boy Scout tricks which go to make the soldier. Each Company now produced a hundred men to march thirty-six miles across the hills in Scale 'A' equipment with no stragglers, and Scale 'A' meant shirt, trousers, bush hat, or cap comforter, big pack containing cardigan, water bottle, spare socks and shirt, log line, camouflage and anti-mosquito cream, rubber jungle boots, washing utensils. a chagul for carrying extra water, and emergency rations. Ammunition was slung round our waists or carried in pouches, and consisted of three hand grenades, two full Bren gun magazines, and a hundred rounds per rifle or Tommy gun. Distributed somewhere else were twenty two-inch mortar bombs, discharger cups, and Verey pistol cartridges. And every man carried if possible a kukri in addition to his tin-opening jack knife. A knife of some sort eventually proved invaluable, whether for cutting down wood for cooking-fires, or felling young trees to protect one's slit trench or slicing the throat of the occasional Japanese who refused to die any other way.

Owing to the habit of enemy snipers of picking officers off if we carried the traditional walking stick and eye-glass, we were dressed exactly as the men except that we had a few extras like torches, compasses, map cases, and a pointer staff, and all these had to be tucked away somewhere.

I had my own idiosyncracies in that I loathed the basic

pouches and instead wore my own, and I always carried a grenade in the trouser pocket meant for field dressings, a short knife which served every purpose from opening sardine tins to cleaning my teeth, and sometimes—just in case of accidents—a flask of any available fire-water.

Of course in action packs might be dumped for a brief battle and kit lightened to the minimum for a short patrol, but for fighting away from secure bases and miles from anything but mule tracks we had to learn to carry on our own backs everything we might need. Many were the arguments waged between the advantages of food, clothing, and ammunition until Scale 'A' was finally 'standardized' or—according to the troops—until the staff could think of nothing more for us to carry.

But time in this story is outstripping space, because many weeks were still to pass before we really had need for the ammunition item of our equipment. In fact I must even confess we had time to enjoy ourselves. There were gymkhanas and Rugby matches, Saturday night outings to the Club in Shillong, the celebration of our Battalion Arroyo Day in October, and the feast of Dashera with the 1/7 and 2/5 Gurkhas in November. At this last we watched the Nepalese dances while rum flowed out of teapots like water down the Thames. But they say others are more competent to write of that night than I, and in case someone does I merely state in self-defence that I did not miss the P.T. parade at 7 o'clock next morning though I may have been throughout approximately one exercise behind the rest. But the Gurkhas are very hospitable people, and perhaps their teapots were responsible.

However, the weeks soon passed. General Cowan assembled all officers and told us 'the Division will assemble forthwith along its operational axis'. This at least meant 'summat was oop', and when on the following Sunday we held a Divisional Church Parade it did not need the Padre's text of 'Confirm the weak hands, and strengthen the feeble knees' to warn us that the march was about to begin.

The mule men and their charges left first, marching by night when the roads were empty, to cover on foot the best part of a thousand miles, and early one morning the rest of the Battalion in jeeps or three-tonners pulled out of the big parade ground, out of Shillong, and finally out of Assam into Manipur and Burma.

We were off to the wars!

*   *   *

This is the story of my Company as I remember it through those years, and if I do not keep mentioning individuals by name it is because their individual stories would detract from the whole, and not because I cannot remember their faces or the parts they played. I had commanded 'B' Company longer than the other Company Commanders, my N.C.O.s were entirely of my own training, and I had contrived to keep together a surprisingly large proportion of the original men from the Cumberland days.

This was a very important factor when reinforcements to the Battalion had been, and continued to be, drawn from men of any Regiment and with varied standards of training. It was a great pity men had to be sent abroad at this time without the hope of Regimental loyalties to inspire their postings. The Army, like all other authoritative bodies in Britain, comes in for much abuse from its members. But its Regiments are sacred, and many a soldier has held on in a tough situation because of the strength of that local pride. The talk of belonging to the best Platoon, of the finest Company, of the crack Battalion, of *THE* Regiment, means something much more real to the soldier than the fact that he is enlisted in the British Army—a body which apparently consists of licentious morons in peacetime but of noble-minded heroes when war begins. We had posted to us later men who had been through no fewer than six different Regiments, and it was small wonder that their attitude was 'What flaming nonsense have I got to stomach in this flaming mob?' That attitude was eventually softened by time and experience, but something was bound to be lacking in the vital confidence of the Platoon or Company concerned if, as so often happened, those reinforcements arrived while the Battalion was in or near action.

Yet, as I have already said, we had contrived to keep our 'B' Company ranks fairly intact, to the eternal mystification of the Adjutant—a being who, screened behind unfathomable depths of paper, existed apparently for the sole purpose of disrupting just such a scheme.

I had only one regular Sergeant. But the others—Little, Carter, Irving, Larke—were as brave, loyal, and hard-working as could be found anywhere. Little for instance had bought himself out of the Regular Army three years before the war, and had come home from India to get married. As a Reservist he was immediately called up again, and he put all his Cumberland toughness into turning us all into soldiers. I remember as a subaltern trying to teach his Platoon the art of silent movement. Whilst we fell out for the 'ten minutes' smoke', without which no soldier works for long, he crawled off on his own and came back with a rabbit he had caught with his bare hands. Once I went to say good-bye to his wife at Carlisle, and was introduced to two charming little daughters who kept inserting into their baby conversation the most surprising oaths. '—me, sir!' said Sergeant Little, 'I can never understand where the little —s learn their bad language!' 'B' Company may have learnt some too, but they also learnt from him much fieldcraft which saved many a life long after he himself fell to a sniper's shot near Vanglai.

The three Platoons in 'B' Company always had very distinct characteristics. 10 Platoon started with plenty of material and with no confidence in itself or in its N.C.O.s, but thanks largely to Arnold Schlund (who took them over in March 1942) they became in the end the least spectacular but the soundest of the lot. If 11 Platoon were always flashy and if they made far more mistakes than the rest of the Company, they had a habit of making a brilliant recovery—like marching on a completely wrong compass bearing, only to find they had stumbled on an enemy headquarters when they got there. In action they proved incredibly brave. 12 Platoon were the 'old soldiers'. Not that any of them really were, but from the start they had a flair for appearing experienced in all they did and they bore out their reputation by their unruffled behaviour under fire.

Company Headquarters were a clique who could at least always be relied upon for humour, even when they were having to run messages or tap on the wireless set while the rest were smoking or 'brewing up'. There was a farmer, a tailor, a banker, a shipbuilder, and a professional boxer, and I doubt if any of them settled easily in their old jobs after the war. However much the long parting from their homes has grieved them, however unpleasant the conditions under which we often lived, something was gained in sharing it all, and it was a something which could be gained in no other way.

The many discussions on Green's future wedding, the joke Pte. Precious would ruefully produce when he brought some unusually irksome news from Battalion Headquarters, Bates's cockney methods of dealing with his temperamental mule, Dade, the Company Clerk, with his encyclopaedic knowledge of everything connected with the numbers, names, addresses, and records of the hundred and eighteen men who comprised the Company, these things will be remembered long after we have forgotten the whine of a bullet, the soreness of our feet, and even the taste of a soya link sausage.

Such were my thoughts as the dawn light grew from grey to red, from red to brilliant blue, and the Battalion convoy curled eastward out of Shillong in search of its 'operational axis'.

V

THE ROAD

That convoy set off with as many instructions as if it were crossing the Atlantic, so many miles in the hour, so many vehicles to the mile, so many look-outs per vehicle, so many Bren guns to be manned for A.A., so many sentries to be posted at halts, so many minutes to be allowed for 'brewing up', so many more rules which were made to be broken.

The first breakage occurred before we left Shillong. Officers were allowed to take sixty pounds of kit, and that should have left room in my jeep for the driver, my batman, and the C.S.M. I had pretended to take great interest in the packing situation, and the decisions regarding which favourite garments were to be left behind. In fact, Green made all the decisions, and when I got to the jeep after having seen the Company into its lorries I found him seated high on a mound of kit at the back with a disconsolate-looking Sergeant-Major standing alongside. It was too late to do anything about it. The C.S.M. was persuaded he would travel much more comfortably in a three-tonner, and we set off. I think the C.O. never discovered why I had more clean clothes than anyone else, or how 'B' Company smuggled a gramophone into the Chin Hills.

The troops all travelled in open three-tonners, twenty men in each plus their kit and some ammunition. It was not a comfortable way of journeying for ten days, especially as one of the features of The Road was its unavoidable dust, and in consequence a band of pathetic-looking white-faced minstrels used to clamber out at every halt.

From Shillong the route started due north, towards Gauhati and then turned sharply eastwards along the Brahmaputra, winding through the hills of Assam. I think many of us felt the significance of that turn. We began to enter a part of the earth dominated by the landscape and not by its inhabitants. Signs of human occupation became rarer and rarer, and even the animals were dangerous rather than friendly. Previously we had always had a civilized base within reach, and we had never been far from roads, aerodromes, and railways, but now our lifeline was the slender link of the Tiddim road, carved by the mad urges of war into a country which till then had barely known a footpath.

So the dusty days passed, and we began to feel more and more oriented forward. Our road now was the road to Burma, to Mandalay, and to Rangoon. There was welcome in that country only for those who had strength to conquer, and surely we could never come back along those dusty miles.

I remember too the feeling of having left civilization behind when our convoy parked for the night after its first hundred miles. We were in a small friendly town. We had spent many a night in the open before, but as each Company was allotted its area of dried mud to sleep on and as the individual mosquito nets began to blossom on their bamboo sticks I realized once and for all that beds, pillows, and pyjamas were things of an already distant past and that the essentials for a good night's rest in future were a blanket, a piece of dry ground, and no disturbances.

On the second night we stopped by a river in which, before we had our bully stew, we sluiced off the layers of dust. The officers' 'Mess', consisting of a few tins and bottles in a trailer, had twice broken loose from its jeep during the day, and it was unanimously condemned as overloaded. It was a warm and starry evening as we sat round a hurricane lamp sipping from tin mugs and mess tins. Several remarked how the warmth and stars increased as the bottles were emptied, and the trailer was considerably lighter next day.

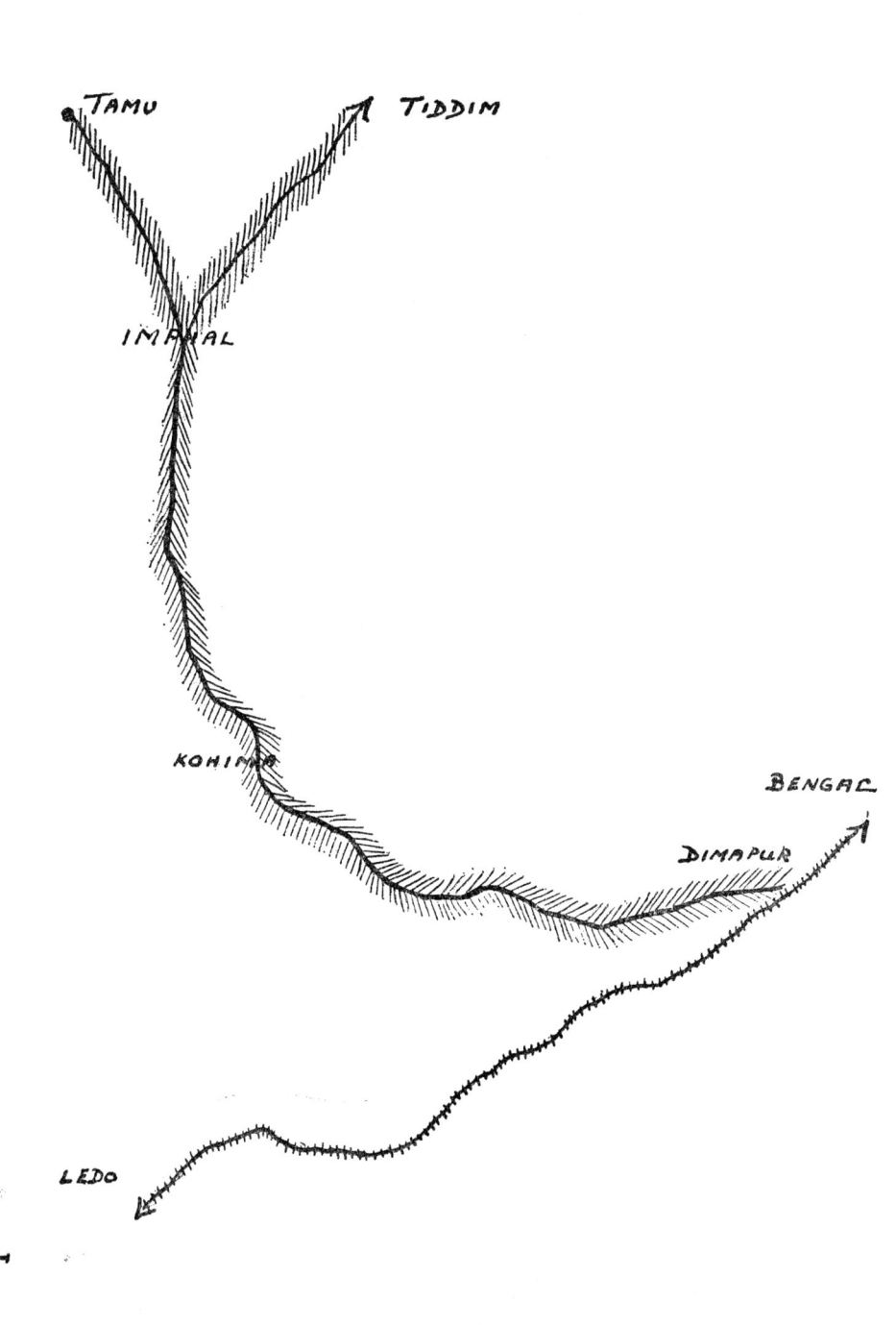

Our next stop was at Dimapur, the railhead of the narrow-gauge railways which supplied the whole Burma front. But we saw little of it because we had orders to be on the road before light, and by 03.30 hrs. the Company was lining up in the dark for its breakfast of porridge, bread and bacon.

British officers spend a lot of time supervising troops' feeding, and we were now getting the value of some of the slick tricks learnt in training for the organization of meals in the field. The C.Q.M.S. together with my Second-in-Command or a Platoon Commander supervised every meal, and each Section Commander reported his Section through—or so many absent on duty—before he fed himself. With one hundred and twenty men to be fed without lights several hours before dawn some such system was necessary to ensure everyone got one helping and nobody got two.

From Dimapur The Road really started. It was no longer flanked by river or railway, and from now on it had to carry the troops and supplies which made our forward army. The value of the air route to Imphal was as yet unmeasured.

The one hundred and sixty miles of Road which wound over the Naga hills and came down to two thousand feet again at the Manipuri capital of Imphal had been broadened and metalled by the time we came to use it, but the countless little culverts and the bridges spanning the steep-sided gorges and the sight of The Road clinging to the sides of the tremendous hills it rounded or overcame gave us plenty of reminders of the troubles which must have faced its engineers of the year before.

Soon after dawn was breaking, and after climbing steadily for nearly four hours we reached Kohima, and here it was cold enough for greatcoats as we turned to take a last look back towards the plains of India. Soon we were over the pass. Warm sunshine spread over the ten thousand foot peak above us and only the Red Crosses shining from the British Hospital on the hillside gave any hint of the blood and battle which would one day ravage the peaceful village on the col behind.

Meanwhile the troops were more interested in tea than in thoughts of war or in the towering ranges which lay around us. 'Brewing up' was being brought to a fine art. Men worked in pairs as in all their jungle training, and one emptied a water bottle into a mess tin and produced tea, sugar, and a tin of milk, while his 'mucker' was busy cutting wood and, at last having found a use for anti-mosquito cream, making the fire. Green broke all records that morning by doing the whole job and producing our 'char' in under fifteen minutes.

It was a glorious morning as we watched 'A' Company's lorries move off. They reappeared, perched apparently over some precipice ahead, and we in our jeep turned our heads at each corner to see our six lorries safely round behind us. For some miles past Kohima the hillside was cut into banked-up rice fields, like the tiers of a wedding cake, and Naga villages could be seen on every spur. But soon there were no signs of habitation except occasional cattle moving in the valley far below or the 'basha' huts in which lived the brightly-clothed ex-head-hunters who were helping to make The Road.

The scenery was superb. The Highlands without heather, the Yorkshire fells without their stone villages, all on a colossal scale which made our trucks look very puny. For once that inexplicable disease which affects all convoys and makes the leading vehicles stifle yawns at fifteen m.p.h. while everyone at the back is tearing madly along at forty failed to grip us, and we moved serenely into the plain of Imphal.

The airstrip had been bombed by the Japanese the day before, and the order had gone forth for slit trenches to be dug at all long halts in future. War was getting nearer, but it was still unknown enough for us to look forward to its thrills. As we passed the fighter planes snuggling into the red hillside I did not foresee the day when I should be flying strapped to a stretcher off that same smooth runway, nor could I guess that many of the men in the lorries behind me would lie in the little cemetery on the other side of the road.

* * *

From Imphal there were two roads to the Burma front. One, broad and metalled, ran south-east to Tamu and faced the Japs only sixty miles away. The other, narrow and dusty, was our road to Tiddim, lying one hundred and sixty miles away up in the Chin Hills. The Japs had already begun to eat their way towards that village from their base at Kalemyo some fifty miles away in the plains. Our forward base was thus supplied by a road, little more than a jeep track as yet, which ran parallel to the Japanese positions along the Chindwin and they could cut it any time they liked to penetrate the sixty-odd miles of tangled hills which lay between.

However, we did not bother much about the strategy when we set off the next day after the Colour-Sergeant's usual nightmare of breakfast in the dark. It was a strange Armistice Day that day we first crossed the boundary between India and Burma—November 11, 1943.

Several lorries from H.Q. and 'A' Companies in front broke down and were passed with great difficulty on the narrow road. Convoy disease broke out badly, and I soon gave up trying to keep in touch with the troops ahead. Above all the dust was with us again and soon lay inches thick on everything, from the Colonel's moustache to the two sardines each of us had for lunch. It seemed to rise upward like steam from some foetid crack in the floor of the jungle, but fortunately no enemy aeroplanes had yet taken to strafing so clearly-etched a target.

Milestones were now our landmarks in a land without villages, and we stopped that night at M.S. 98. Here for the first time fires had to be screened and movement hidden from possible prying eyes on the next big ridge that framed the skyline. We had reached the road limit of three-tonners now, and after a night spent sorting some very muddled kit we marched down to the river at M.S. 109. It was then an unkempt basha camp, but later to become a hospital and base for all kinds of stores.

We were supposed to stay at M.S. 109 for a week to get our 'hill legs' on some of the local test climbs and generally clean up ourselves and our weapons once more, but it was not to be. We spent one day in the river trying to dye our underclothes that 'jungly' colour with a mixture of local berries and potassium permanganate and in listening to a reassuring lecture on future operations from the Brigadier, and then at ten o'clock the following morning we were told the Japs were attacking our positions in force at Fort White, twenty-two miles from Tiddim, and we were ordered to march out at midday.

M.S. 109 was deep in the valley, and we were soon sweltering as we marched straight into the afternoon sun and round the shoulder of a great mountain, nicked as ever by frequent nullahs which added many miles to our route. With very sore feet we camped that night at M.S. 126 and bathed in the moonlight under the suspension bridge which spanned the fast-flowing Manipur river.

The Battalion was under half an hour's notice to move and we slept while we could. Fortunately the jeeps did not arrive till dawn to fetch us. The Indian boys who drove them had been on the move all night but they seemed refreshed enough by a spit and a smoke, and with five of us to a jeep and all our kit as usual on our backs 'B' Company set off as Advance Guard on the last lap of the journey.

The Road was narrower and dustier than ever, and as full of thrills as any scenic railway—and not nearly as safe! Sometimes we had to dig our way through piles of rubble fallen from above, sometimes, as we looked down through the open side of the jeep we could see tracks ploughed down hundreds of feet through the jungly hillside by some previous driver who had found that even a jeep cannot cling to a mountainside on only two wheels. However after one tricky moment when the jeep in front of me started sliding backwards—and took most of the road with it—we found ourselves by midday tackling the hairpin bends of the 'Chocolate Staircase' which brought us up the last few thousand feet into Tiddim.

This Chin village served as a market centre and meeting-place for the few hundred hillmen who lived their lives within its reach. Like a saddle which has partly slipped off a horse's back it sprawled on both sides of the main ridge and at the top of the four thousand foot spur we had climbed from the Manipur river. Up this spur zigzagged the new road carved crazily from the hillside whose browny-red soil gave the 'staircase' its name.

It was a town peaceful men had made, yet now it belonged to intruders with gas-masks and swinging scabbards and clumsy boots and spluttering engines. Most of its younger men had already gone, many to join the Burma Rifles, and it was not easy to pretend to such villagers as remained—the old or the very young—that we too had homes and gardens and children who had to be protected from lorry wheels. Nor, sadly, do I recall feeling the need to try.

As we rounded the last corner of that fierce climb the cross of a small Mission church appeared below. How could we explain that ours too was a Christian path which led us to take from these people their fields and homes—Tiddim was burned to the ground by us within the year—and to lord it over their lives and deaths? For generations the cattle bells had sounded on those hills and the rice had grown and withered in the valleys. But now, like a nut between crackers, Tiddim lay where East met West, and the day had come when the shape of its contours and the lines of its approaches mattered between nations.

But I was not left to ponder long. Our Indian jeep driver, brave beyond his knowing at the task he had just completed, was pointing away up to the left where we could imagine our Gurkhas digging in on Kennedy Peak. It was still fourteen miles on along the track ahead, but the Jap might come by several ways and the driver kept peering anxiously into the jungle slopes around us. And I, feeling rather lonely, remembered the Battalion which lay behind us down the road.

VI

THE CHIN HILLS

Both sides at this stage of the war—that is in the months just after the 1943 monsoon—were busy building their strength for further advances. The British were only just beginning to spare supplies from their commitments in the Middle East; the Japanese according to their propaganda were getting ready to invade India. Meanwhile there had been no large-scale offensive action since the original Burma Army had broken contact in 1942, but this did not mean inaction for the troops left to guard those eastern outposts, because long lonely patrols or short bloody ambushes were constantly taking place somewhere in that tangled mass of hills and jungle. Seventeen Division had made the Chin Hills their battleground from the start and were faced by their old enemies the Japanese Thirty-third, one of the crack Divisions from the original Burma fighting.

The battleground was tremendous in every detail. In the days of peace you could have reached Tiddim from Rangoon by Irrawaddy steamer and the still undefiled Chindwin Valley. But the Army's road had of necessity been driven across the grain of the country, and now we were climbing its final ridge. This ridge was the backbone of the Chin Hills, and I must explain that the milestones start afresh at Tiddim. The Road turned east at Milestone 8 and after rounding Vital Corner at Milestone 14 wound southwards over Kennedy Peak. Becoming more and more a mere jeep track and with thick steep jungle on one side and open precipitous nullahs on the other it clung to the undulating ridge top till it passed just below the

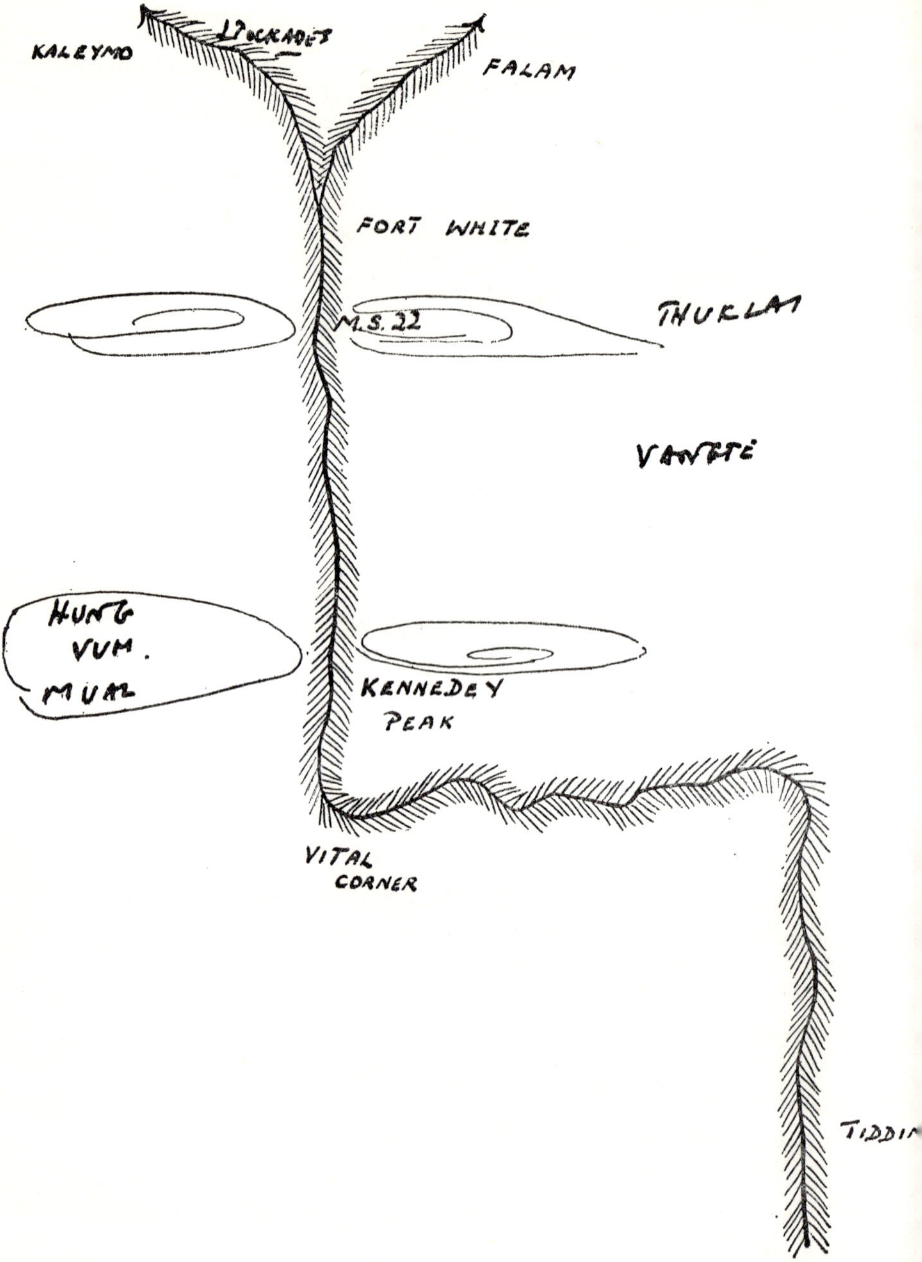
KALEYMO
STOCKADES
FALAM
FORT WHITE
M.S. 22
THUKLAI
HUNG
VUM.
MUAL
KENNEDEY
PEAK
VITAL
CORNER

Jap-held crest of Milestone 22, and then, taking in the few bungalows which comprised Fort White, it dropped rapidly eastwards past the old Stockade position—where 17 Division had already won its first V.C.—and sank down to Kalemyo and the Chindwin port of Kalewa and so on to the purple plains of central Burma.

Away to the west and beyond the Manipur river trackless ranges lay between us and the fighting in the coastal district of the Arakan.

To the east several vast ridges provided footpaths to the plains seven thousand feet below, and wherever these ridges narrowed and rose to a dominating mountain there sat the little Nips from Tokio to bar our path. In the fighting which had just brought us flapping up from M.S. 109 they had captured just such a position dominating the one possible route on the near side of Fort White. This was the famous M.S. 22, against which we were destined to beat our heads in vain for the next six months. A Battalion of the Punjab Regiment, weak in numbers, and 'borrowed' from another Division was caught there in penny packets by the Japs, who attacked at night through the thickest part of the jungle.

So our Brigade arrived at Tiddim to find itself committed initially to defence. 63 Brigade had fallen back on Kennedy Peak and Vital Corner, and we were to protect Tiddim and its western approaches.

On such an immense landscape it felt like defending the Alps with a Platoon, and there could be no continuous line of defence. Companies or Battalions were just at intervals along The Road, sometimes with several miles separating them. It was the old theory of all-round defence applied to the smallest unit, and an enemy could easily infiltrate between the perimeters. So what? He was as surrounded as we were—provided we stood firm and saved our ammunition. The more important positions were wired, and all were booby-trapped with punjis (sharpened bamboo spikes) and 36 grenades, except of course at the used entrances.

In my first Company position about three miles south of Tiddim our preliminary scratchings in the approved weapon-pit style and the leafy bowers we built alongside to sleep in were more suited to a performance of *As You Like It* than fighting the Japanese. However we crawled about carefully in the undergrowth wielding our entrenching tools. The Japs were still twenty miles away, but we had always been taught one is never safe in the jungle. Fortunately we got initiated into our war by slow degrees, and we also had the advantage of learning all the tricks from Gurkha troops who had been playing the game for several years.

The standard 'bunker', with which all our perimeters were eventually manned, was a two-man model and consisted of a trench in which both men could stand to shoot and a couch of earth and stones upon which one could lie to sleep. It was roofed with logs to a thickness of about four feet and since grenades could not be thrown through the narrow slits a firing bay was also dug outside, for use when the enemy got really close. All night and every night one of the two men kept watch, two hours on and two hours off, linked to the watchers on his right and left by a 'telephone' made of creeper tied to a tin-can full of stones.

In jungle fighting, as in night fighting, there was little section control or text-book fire orders. Once the party started those two men stayed and fought on their own, depending on the rest while they lived to do the same.

The officer, doing his occasional rounds at night and stopping for a whispered chat through the sacking door of bunkers, had time to reflect on the littleness of our war compared with the black velvet shapes of the great hills around. The soldier, staring out into the vast silence hour after hour and wondering if he heard the crackle of a footstep or the click of a detonator —wondering in many cases what a Japanese looked like anyway—found little to admire even in those innumerable masses of tropical stars or the pale brilliance of the Burma moon.

However foolproof the defences and however overwhelming

the weapons which lay behind them, it was upon the eyes and ears and wills of Privates Brown, Robinson, and the rest that we all relied, and people who try to calculate the sacrifices of war would do well to remember the eternal wearying watches of the infantryman.

It was not easy at first to live strenuously at eight thousand feet, especially when even to get a bath we had to descend to the Manipur river four thousand feet below. This was a trip we made mostly for the exercise and for the fish to be collected when a grenade dropped 'accidentally' into the river. The effect of the bath was somewhat nullified by having to re-climb the equivalent of Ben Nevis afterwards.

The temperature in the river valleys and deep nullahs was tropical. On the hills upon which we lived it was ideal by day but cold enough by night to need a blanket and greatcoat, although we always had to sleep in boots and clothes.

The Road was so congested a lifeline that a great part of our bulk supplies of food and ammunition were dropped by air. One sunny Sunday morning we were watching the slowly circling Dakotas and the white mushrooms of the parachutes bellying beneath them. In other words our beans and bullets were floating gently down to Tiddim. Suddenly something like an angry wasp whizzed over the eastern skyline, in a flurry of cannon fire revealed itself as a Zero fighter, and for a few minutes played with the Dakotas like a shark in a bathing pool.

Our one Bofors gun had been dug in on top of Kennedy Peak and was being much publicized by our S.E.A.C. newspaper as the Highest Anti-aircraft Gun in the World. Its crew in their daily gun-drill shot from the sky any enemy aircraft which dared to approach and at least in theory knew how to fill every yard of that blue sky with bursts—except, alas, those few feet behind and below its position. And that was where the Zero buzzed. Poor Highest Gun, the Zero sped home the way it had come and left a muzzle pointing sadly upwards to await a happier day.

But that was the only hostile aeroplane we saw over the Chin Hills in six months, and though we took normal precautions in spacing mules or troops on the road and were very careful not to collect in large parties for meals we could run risks greater than the armies in the Desert or Western Europe would have dared, and in consequence life was a lot easier.

For instance if we were not involved we could sit comfortably in the open (at a seemly distance from the General and the two Brigadiers) while we watched an attack on a hilltop, only two or three miles away as the shells flew. On reconnaissance in those early days and while we were learning the new names for this unchristened territory I could sit in the shade on an O.P. and point out to N.C.O.s the enemy's positions and our own as simply as if we were still on a scheme on the Northumberland moors, more simply in fact, because there was no all-powerful umpire to creep up on us and say 'You've all been wiped out by enemy aircraft'. How fortunate it is

O.P. Kennedy Peak.

that the deadly accuracy and unlimited ammunition of umpires' weapons are seldom to be found in actual battle!

After about a fortnight of digging and of practising counter-attacks, and of patrolling the 'back door' to Tiddim without seeing a single enemy, we had a sharp reminder that war meant death as well as discomfort. A Chin villager brought in news that six men from the Battalion Commando Platoon had been enticed into a house in a village called Thuklai on the ridge running westward from M.S. 22 and there surprised and bayoneted by the Japanese. One had escaped but had died of his wounds, and the village itself had now been occupied by a Headquarters and some two hundred of the enemy. A raid by a Gurkha Battalion on M.S. 22 had already been planned for next day at dawn, and the Brigadier called for a Platoon from 'B' Company to create a diversionary attack against Thuklai one hour earlier.

It was no great battle, but it is worth noting for several reasons. It was the first time our troops had been committed to definite action against the Japanese, and although I was glad the Platoon came from my Company it felt like sending off a leg without the body when that evening the rest of us saw off 12 Platoon with Sergeant Little and 'Johnty' Johnstone in command. Starting at five o'clock in the evening and with necessary halts only, and travelling throughout on paths, that Platoon got within range of its objective only five minutes before its zero hour of 05.30 hrs. next morning. Twelve and a half hours for fifteen miles gives some indication of the difficulty of the country and the standard of fitness required from troops who had to be fit to fight at the end of such a march. Incidentally a Platoon on such a job would have its two-inch mortar and bombs and two of its Bren guns with reserve ammunition carried on two mules, but even so Scale 'A' was no easy weight to carry up and down hills all night. The premium placed on good map-reading is to be noted next, because one mistake that night and 12 Platoon would have been late and failed in its job.

The fourth and final point is that during this raid the first few dozen of many thousands of later shells were fired on M.S. 22. 'B' Company's leafy dell had suddenly been invaded by a battery of twenty-five pounders one night the week before, and a gun on its jeep axle had even been hauled up on Kennedy Peak itself. Eventually we had medium guns in action near Tiddim, but in those early days the sight of a Field gun on that fantastic road was a surprising and heartening sight.

12 Platoon were due to pull back some miles to a village called Vangte after their show, and I went out with a patrol to take them food and blankets. As we scouted round corners and across the streams en route I alternated between wondering whether I should find a triumphant Platoon with two hundred yellow prisoners or merely a couple of mules to tell the story. Actually they were all there with mess tins brewing on the fire and only a few extra blisters for their trouble. Their orders had been to make a noise like a whole Battalion attacking and then pull out before light to an ambush position, and they had done this with little opposition. 'B' Company could talk at last about having been Under Fire. . . .

On the way back from Vangte we lost our first mule. Bates was trying to lead his much-abused animal past the wrong side of a jeep when the edge of the road gave way, and the mule fell to break its neck a thousand feet below. As some consolation to poor Bates it was at least out of reach of anyone trying to supplement the fresh meat ration, and we certainly realized its living value when its load had to be split up between us.

In the second week of December our Brigade moved up to take over from 63 Brigade who were to make an all-out attack on M.S. 22. There were three main positions forward. We took over Kennedy Peak itself, 1/7 Gurkha Rifles were responsible for Vital Corner (so called because once rounded by the Japs Tiddim was at their mercy), and 2/5 Royal Gurkha Rifles went into a 'box' with the Brigade Headquarters at M.S. 12.

'B' Company took the very top of the Peak as its part of the perimeter—and I became the highest Company Commander in the world. On the maps we were shown as at eight thousand eight hundred feet while the R.A.F. put it at least a thousand feet higher. But no attempt to limit the noughts was made by the troops as they panted their way to the top.

Once round Vital Corner the atmosphere was in many ways less sheltered. Shells bursting on the jungle-covered hilltop of M.S. 22 reminded us that we were face to face with the Japs, even though they were still some seven miles away and too polite as yet to reply. At nine thousand feet climate and the vegetation were different too. Long twiny creepers and thick moss clothed the trees which covered the eastern slopes and which seemed to grow even thicker and more jungly down the nullahs and spurs which linked us to the plains. That Promised Land was often now obscured by cloud through which the sun shone like an occasional spotlight on flat rice fields, on the black speck of a boat on the river Mytha, sometimes even on the sparkling Chindwin or Irrawaddy flowing each in the broad valleys far beyond.

There was usually a wind blowing, and this made it coolish except at midday—and frosty by night. Sometimes as the cigarettes were lighted and talk broke out again after the dawn Stand-down a great red sun rose over a belt of cloud, unbroken save for the peaks of the highest mountains which stood out like black icebergs in a frozen sea. To the Japanese it must have seemed symbolical of their own rising sun triumphant over Burma. But for us—if we thought of it at all —there was comfort in the reflection that the warmth of later hours would dissolve that stifling cloudbank and once more bring light to the land beneath.

Kennedy Peak fast developed from a bare bastion into a tremendously strongly fortified area which could hold two Battalions, and it was remarkable how relatively comfortable we became once the wiring and crawl trenches were finished and there was time to settle in. This was partly because any

Gurkha can build a house with every modern convenience provided he has enough bamboo, and a kukri.

Water was our chief trouble, and the mules had a two-hour journey to bring up the daily supply. But gradually a big reserve was built up in tarpaulin tanks, by bringing it up in oil drums on jeeps from a water-point down the road. Next an underground casualty clearing station was built, also two large officers' messes. Chairs and tables were of bamboo, and the wallpaper and tablecloth of sacking, but we could do very nicely on the settee in front of the mud fireplace, provided the wind was blowing the right way and the smoke went up the chimney, just the same.

Ersatz Bathroom. HQ Coy Kennedy Peak. Made with an oil drum, petrol tins, and sacks.

Another feat of construction was the chapel. Its walls and seats were made like all the rest of bamboo held together by creeper, and its interior had some extraordinarily beautiful touches. The altar cloth and the curtains round the rush-framed windows were made of mosquito netting which had been dyed red from berries to match the rhododendron flowers on the altar. These had been plucked from the surrounding trees, which were then providing a splash of colour in contrast to the eternal green of the jungle, and whatever link with home there might have been for men fighting a pagan enemy in an Asiatic country was surely to be found in the unique sentimentality of that lovely little place.

St Andrews-on-the-Hill

Religion is supposed to be intensified in war. Religion in any theological sense I doubt, but easier appreciation of another world or at least of the existence of forces beyond man's control probably is. The types whose superficial religion depended upon easy church-going found they had little foundation on which to rely when their Sundays were not their own, and when churches were not just round the corner. Another point worth remembering is that, while the Battalion Padre was almost always Church of England, the majority of troops—at least in our North Country Regiment—who called themselves Church of England chose that designation in preference to the established alternative of 'religion: nil'. Apart from Roman Catholics most genuine cases were Nonconformists whose narrower creeds could not be catered for. I was saddened at the way in which those men who felt deeply about their religion objected so strongly to the prayer-book flavour of the Church parade on board ship and at such other places where all had to be present. They took the attitude that 'C. of E.' was 'the snobs' religion, and they were only slightly mollified when a series of brilliant sermons on the *Orcades* turned out to have been broadcast by a Methodist Padre on board.

I couldn't help wondering whether our Christmas Day service on Kennedy Peak provided an example of the unreality of or the nearness of religion to the life we were leading. A Platoon of mine had gone out the night before to lay an ambush near the Japanese positions on M.S. 22, and the rattle of automatics and the smoky puffs of mortar bombs in the distance showed that death as well as birth was in the air that morning as we sat on the hillside singing carols.

* * *

Two days later the Battalion moved back for a rest to M.S. 12, and 'B' Company's casualties after six weeks in contact with the enemy were still nil.

At M.S. 12 we formed a separate 'box' with the Brigade Headquarters, but we were really in reserve to our two Battalions which occupied the more important positions further forward. So by day we trained or rested or helped to widen the road, and by night each company took it in turn to relax.

A surprising amount of Christmas fare had been sent to us up The Road, or had been dropped out of the skies, and we decided to have our delayed Christmas feast on New Year's Eve.

We had our beer and bird and beans before it got dark, and then, while we sat round two enormous wood fires, the organization of the Company concert dissolved at approximately the same rate as the fortnight's rum issue, which had been saved up for the occasion. It was a good party—from the moment when our seventeen-stone Quartermaster, unaware he was sitting on a burning log, sang 'We'll all be merry and bright'—to the early hour of the morning when I found no fewer than three forlorn soldiers searching hopefully in the cold ashes for their false teeth!

A fortnight passed. The Battalions changed again, and this time we went to Vital Corner. So 1944 began and, to prevent my narrative from digressing as if written in the haze of New Year's Eve, I shall group our Chin Hill activities under the two main headings of 'Patrolling' and 'Attacks on M.S. 22'.

VII

PATROLLING

Patrolling was a feature of life in the Chin Hills, whatever position the Battalion was holding. Sometimes a fighting patrol a Platoon strong, sometimes merely an officer and his orderly, there would always be somebody lying out in the shade to watch a jungle track by day or moving silently under the stars by night. When there was no definite reconnaissance on hand the favourite and most usual was a Tiger Patrol of two men who, armed with Tommy guns and grenades, would try to catch the Japs in the open and spread as much consternation and destruction as possible before disappearing again into the jungle. It sounds easy. But the Jap seldom stirred out of his main positions, and it took plenty of nerve for two men to attack in country where even a broken ankle might mean starvation in the jungle or capture by an enemy who was governed by no rules in his treatment of prisoners.

It would be wearisome to record all this constant and unsung warfare, and I shall now describe the details of one patrol which combined the aspects of most.

By March 1944, the Battalion was still one or two down in casualties in comparison with those inflicted on the Japs, and in particular no yellow prisoner had yet been taken. Companies as such were engaged in few operations, and four longish patrols planned by Brigade were played for by eager Company Commanders, who were themselves to go out 'to keep their eye in'.

My poker was not up to standard in this gamble, and it was only after three abortive attempts that my show appeared on the programme. I was always against picking special teams for these outings, and since 11 Platoon were without an officer and had been having one of their bad spells I chose twenty-five of them—plus two mule-men, my own batman, and two stretcher-bearers.

The scene was set on the great ridge which broke off eastward from Kennedy Peak and reached the plains some twenty miles away. The Japanese had two positions to bar this route, one at a place called Pimpi on a branch of the main ridge, the other on a hill known by its spot height as 4392 and above the village of Dollouang and about six miles short of the plains. A good mule track was marked on the map, and it was thought it might be possible to put a careless little Nip into the bag, while he brought up supplies to the Dollouang position or sauntered back towards the plains. A nice easy scheme on the map in the Brigadier's office, but I felt it unlikely we could ever drag a wounded prisoner back over the sort of country we would have to face.

Anyway we set off in good heart, if for no other reason than because I had permission to be away for two whole weeks. We were going to be on our own and not even connected by wireless to Battalion Headquarters—from whose worrying but necessary grip it was always pleasant to be free.

The idea was to have a base near enough to Dollouang to do the job, and one in which we could safely leave some of the heavier things we carried. A reconnaissance would be necessary first, and I set off with a section of seven men, mules carrying a blanket for each of us, and enough tinned rations for fourteen days.

We set off in daylight from Vital Corner. Our path to begin with had been well and recently patrolled, and we were soon outside the Kennedy Peak perimeter, moving in single file down and through the thick jungle which covered its eastern slope.

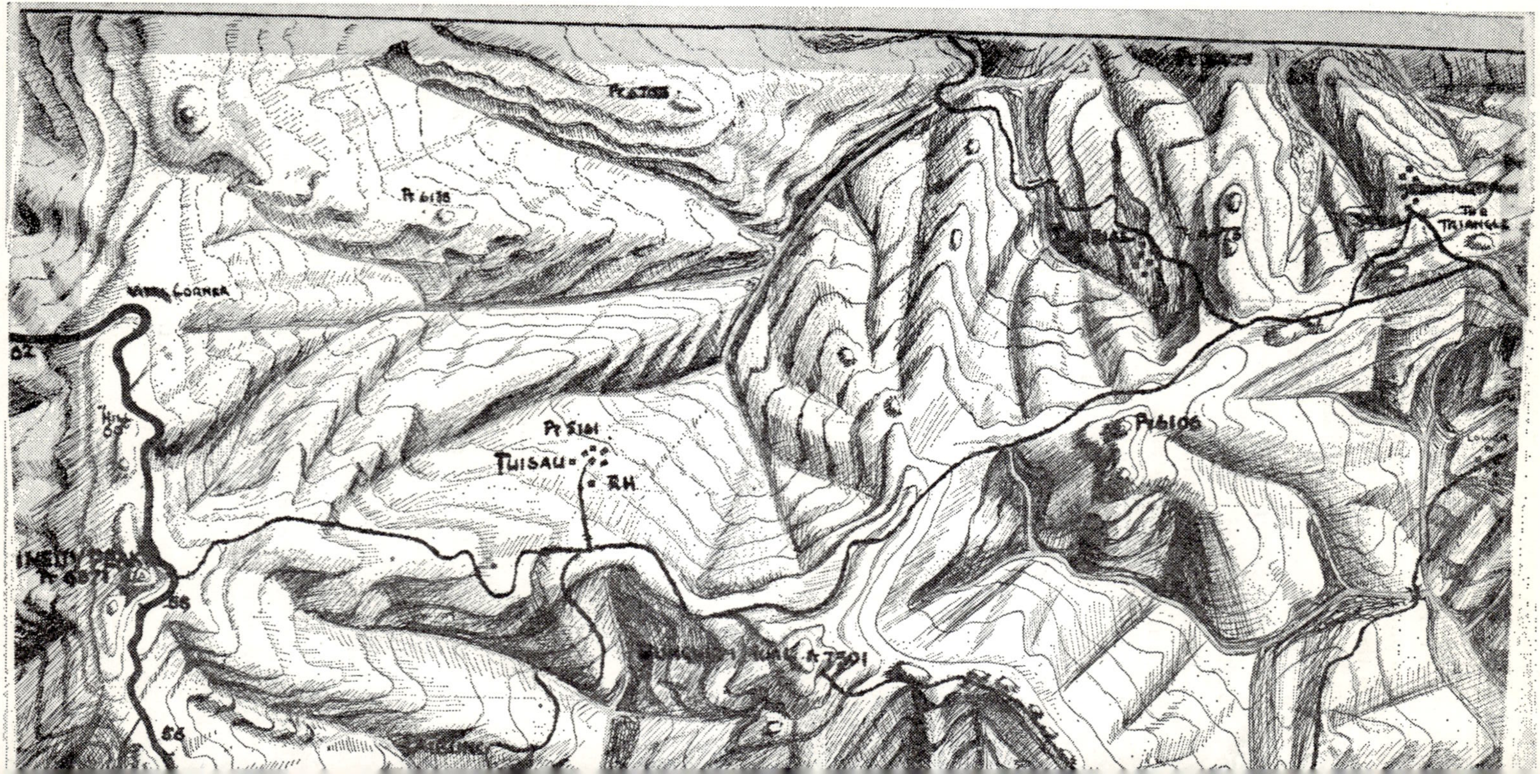

Pt 6138
Pt 5161
TUISAU
R.H.
Pt 6106
THE TRIANGLE

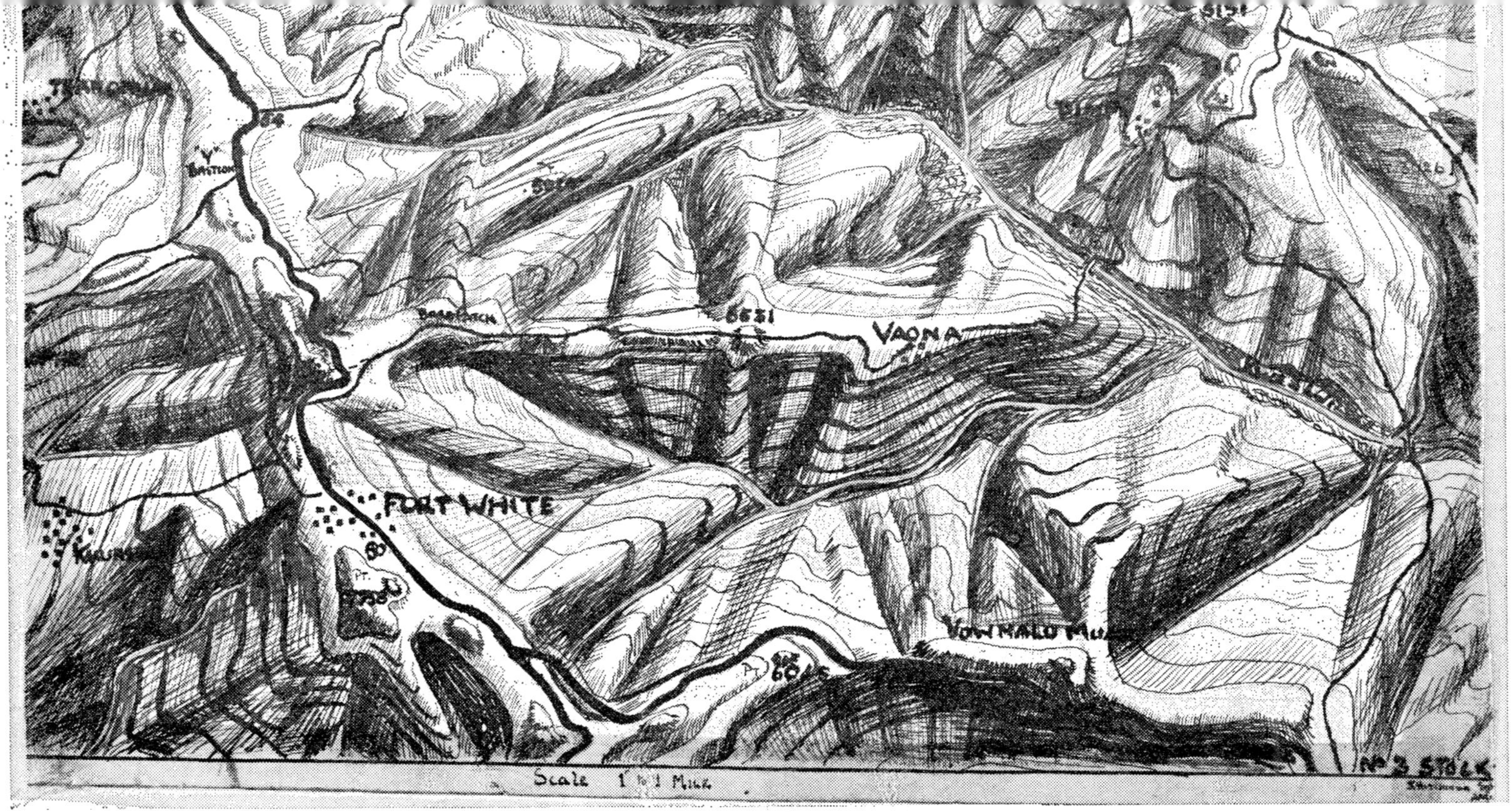
FORT WHITE
VAONA
6531
Scale 1" to 1 Mile

A Platoon order of march, which was the same in degree for other bodies, consisted of two scouts marching ahead at visibility distance from the leading Section. Its small headquarters came next, followed by the mules and the other two Sections. Finally two men kept some thirty or forty yards behind the rear Section, and at times another pair was pushed out to a flank. Frequent Company Battle Drills of the past would, we hoped, prevent lack of control if we bumped into the enemy, and an Emergency Rendezvous was arranged every few hours in case we had to scatter. In thick jungle without landmarks this rendezvous would often be so many hundred yards ahead and in the direction the enemy would least expect us.

Messages to call up Section Commanders to look out for a sniper, to form up for a 'Blitz' or to disperse right or left were all made by signals. After not raising one's voice for a fortnight it is difficult to get out of the habit, and I have several times returned from a long patrol and surprised everyone by continuing to talk in a whisper.

At one point our path came out into the open on the side of the ridge, and might have been under observation from the Japanese on M.S. 22; in consequence we had to cut round the back and thus wasted two hours on one of my less successful 'short cuts'. Because of this set-back it was dark when we climbed again round the eight thousand foot shoulder of Hung Vum Mual, and here we parted from Johnty and Sgt. Larke who went off on a reconnaissance of the Jap positions at Pimpi.

After two hours' climb we started to descend again, but because of the delay it was nearly midnight before I could give the signal to halt for the night. This was at a deserted post once held by Chin levies, a desirable spot because it was far enough off the path for reasonable safety and contained some weapon pits in case of alarm, and even more acceptably some ready-made bashas complete with leaf-covered bamboo beds. One of the arts we now had to acquire was to manoeuvre and unload mules in the thick undergrowth and dense blackness of a moonless night. The animals themselves—with the inevitable barbary exception—were admirably silent and surefooted.

Early next morning we moved off, and by ten o'clock we had reached the area of our main base. We chose a spot where a stream crossed the path some two miles short of the Japanese positions above Dollouang on Hill 4392. A hill to the right of the path above our stream rose to 5126 feet, and instead of the rhododendron trees and cooler scrub of Kennedy Peak we found ourselves amongst much thicker and steamier vegetation with areas of fruitless banana palms and occasionally overgrown clearings which before the war had been cultivated by Chin villagers.

It was easy to hide my section of seven, but I knew it would be necessary to move my base by night from anywhere where we might have been seen by day as soon as the rest of the Platoon arrived. I hoped, however, to keep in touch with the stream for our water supply, and at the same time be far enough from the path for us to risk lighting a fire for brewing tea—an evening morale-raiser it took a lot of danger to make us forgo. Provided no suspicions were aroused by noise or smoke or tracks, a Jap patrol would then have to stumble right on us to find us.

I had decided to take just two N.C.O.s, Cpl. Whenray and L/Cpl. Graham, on my preliminary reconnaissance, and we went forward that first afternoon to compare the ground with the route we had studied from the map.

We found an O.P. half a mile away on the forward slope of the Hill 5126, and we got to work with binoculars. Ahead of us the tree-tops swept steeply down to a nullah which ran north to south across our front: a stream junction was marked 2056—that is over three thousand feet below—but the last few hundred feet were so sheer that it was almost impossible to get a glimpse of the water.

To our left ran the continuation of the ridge we had come down, and we could see the path ahead emerging from thick jungle to wind round the right-hand side of 4392's comparatively bare top. Behind 4392 and unseen from our O.P. the ridge continued to the plains, and there lay the path which was to be our objective. To the right of 4392 as we looked at it ran another ridge which formed the far side of the nullah in front of us, and which passed a subsidiary bump—mapped as 4056—about three-quarters of a mile along its spine. Another path could be seen at intervals along the crest of this ridge, and in addition quite a broad red track ran down through Dollouang village. This track continued downhill to the stream junction at 2056, then up again to the other Jap position of Pimpi to our right. The village was shining and looked peaceful enough in the sunlight, but some of its houses were roofless, probably because corrugated iron had been taken for strengthening the bunkers, and we saw no sign of movement on the hill above.

My plan was to reach the far ridge to the right of 4056 by moving down through the jungle to the nullah below, and then we could move left-handed round the back of this position to our objective. The chief dangers seemed to be the steepness of the final drop, the crossing of the Dollouang-Pimpi path, the presence of Japs on 4056, and the nature of the unseen country behind Dollouang ridge. We also had to find a route which would strike the balance between dense jungle and the more open country beyond, because while we waited we did not want to be visible and thus walk into an ambush. Anyway it all looked feasible, and it merely remained to get cracking on the morrow and see what happened.

So back at our base we cleaned weapons and ammunition and finally checked orders and signals, and we were under our blankets as soon as it was dark.

We did not enjoy a good night's rest. Unfortunately we had chosen the night meeting-ground of a herd of enormous hump-backed cattle who insisted, fairly enough, I suppose, that they had first claim to what had seemed a pleasantly flat piece of ground. I remember lying awake while the inquisitive beasts clanked their wooden bells round us and snortingly expressed displeasure at our presence, and, as the hours passed, the hills ahead seemed to get steeper in my thoughts, and the jungles thicker and more Jap-infested.

The three of us moved off soon after light. We were dressed alike in jungle boots, green-coloured slacks and shirts, cap comforters fashioned in our favourite styles, and our faces were painted a mossy hue from camouflage cream. My two N.C.O.s had Tommy guns and kukris while I had a rifle and bayonet and my favourite dagger knife. Each of us carried a grenade and fifty rounds, and I was draped in addition with a compass, map-case, torch, binoculars, and of course the 'medicine' flask. The N.C.O.s carried a blanket apiece with spare socks and cardigans, and I had the rations. For the two days we expected to be away we had a tin of sardines each, a tin of cheese, a small tin of bully, three packets of biscuits, tea, sugar and milk, and—in the hopes of a warm brew—a Tommy cooker. All this may sound a lot to carry on reconnaissance. But we had a long way to go in forty-eight hours and we had proved in the past we couldn't go more lightly clad without feeling very cold, and very hungry, and very unarmed.

After an appalling start through a thicket laced with thick creeper and giant prickly bracken we moved quickly down the spur and by 13.00 hrs. we came to the steep drop overlooking the stream. We could not go straight ahead without starting a minor avalanche, so we worked our way towards it left-handed. The tinkling of the water became louder and louder until it drowned the occasional voices floating across the nullah from Dollouang—now far above us—and the tappings and rustlings in the surrounding jungle. We 'froze' to verify every noise. Ears carry further than eyes in that country, and we could afford no risks when even the crackle of a leaf or the cry of a bird might prove to be a slant-eyed patrol. We had done it so often during training—the front man peering forward, the second on the left, the third right and rear—that even in this apparently innocent jungle we kept expecting to hear the whistle-call with which all good schemes ended.

We hit the stream without finding any way of getting across to the open spur which was our previously chosen landmark and which was now about three miles downstream towards Pt. 2056. We therefore decided to risk using the stream itself and found it on the whole shallow, though many tumbled boulders lurked between its deeper pools.

One at a time we filled our water bottles, the last man smoothing out foot-prints when it was necessary to tread on a patch of gravel in case the distinctive ribbing of our jungle boots should betray us. To avoid leaving trails and traces was a gospel I had preached loud and often to troops normally very careless about it. That I returned from this particular reconnaissance minus a pair of mittens and a handkerchief with my name on it was not one of the better kept secrets of the war, but luckily the handkerchief was marked 'Obolensky' instead of Cooper, and if the Japs ever found it the confirmation of the presence of a Russian patrol in the Burma jungle may have done more good than harm.

At 14.15 hrs. we came upon the Dollouang-Pimpi track, with our powder still dry in spite of one or two slippery moments. The track here crossed the stream by a wooden bridge, and we stopped to watch it for three-quarters of an hour, in the last five minutes of which L/Cpl. Graham saw three Chin villagers pad quietly across on their way home.

They may have been friendly, but in enemy-held country we could trust no one. Since the side of the nullah hereabouts was just negotiable I laid the protractor on the map, and we set off on a compass-bearing through the bamboo jungle on the far side. It was not an easy trip, but at 17.30 hrs. we arrived on the edge of the open spur which we had chosen the day before. The crown of the spur had been cleared for cultivation for half its length, and we had picked it both as a recognizable check on our bearings and because it led directly up to Pt. 4056. We knew we would have to climb this latter in the dark, and we set off again at 19.00 hrs., after a bite of bully and our first—and successful—attempt with the Tommy cooker.

Apart from a few unnecessary detours incurred by stalking the tree stumps and hay stooks which dotted the open spur we moved up smoothly to the fringe of the mile of scrubby jungle on our side of the track which ran along the ridge below 4056. This was our next landmark, and it took us about an hour and a half to reach it. Here we stopped to rest, and I re-set the compass and checked back on a few landmarks in case of coming trouble.

Two of the three adjectives which filled all the troops' conversation at that time were 'smashing' and 'deadly', the acme and nadir of soldiering epithets. For instance the rum ration was usually 'smashing', and the grub 'deadly'. But the view as we looked back that night was both. There was no moon—we had timed it so the party following us would get that—but under the brightness of the star-studded sky the hills looked terrific, crouching black giants with all irregularities smoothed away by the cloak of night. Kennedy Peak and M.S. 22 towered far above us on the top shelf of all; the flat tops of Hung Vum Mual and of Pt. 5126 and the cone of Pimpi dominated the far side of our nullah. Somewhere in that tremendous backcloth lay the little group of men and mules we had left behind that morning, somewhere under Pimpi's cone Sgt. Larke and Johnty lay watching and listening. In fact the scene was 'smashing' and 'deadly' in another way too, because we were looking at land from an angle of sight which the Japanese thought was theirs alone. Indeed, one of their positions was already far behind us.

More important than these thoughts, however, was the opportunity we were given to fix definite landmarks in the west, in case any one of us should be forced to travel back that way, alone and by night.

The patch of jungle ahead was thick and scrubby, and there was actually a path winding through it. But every time it wound our leading man walked straight on into a bush, and we were very scratched and bad-tempered by the time we suddenly came out on a broad path which we assumed to be the one just below the crest of the ridge.

We lay for an hour listening for activity, but all we heard was the dull boom of guns from Kennedy Peak and the crash of shells bursting round and near Dollouang not far away on our left. It was at least a check that we were not yet lost, but it was also a sharp reminder that we were well in enemy territory.

We now set off along the track in an attempt to slip over the ridge to the right of 4056. There was less than half a mile to go, but it was a nasty bit of path. Above us for all we knew an enemy was waiting to get us deeper into his trap, below us and to our right the jungle fell steeply and even more impenetrably towards yet another nullah. The path was covered with dry bamboo leaves which went off like crackers, and with slimy dead ones which might hide a booby-trap. Three times we entered and passed through a gloomy tunnel where the vegetation met above our heads and where white-faced bushes peered at us from the undergrowth while tall bamboo stems tapped out signals as their tops rustled in the breeze. Eventually—though by going too far along the track we had to pull back and climb another path beside a tiny stream—we did cross the ridge in safety, and after we had collected ourselves it was a moot point whether we or the two barking deer we flushed half way up were the more surprised to be alive.

We were in unknown country now, and we lay down to await daylight as soon as we were well below 4056 and could find a relatively flat piece of ground. It was pointless posting a sentry to guard three men. It was far safer to lie still than prowl around, so we packed in a heap on one blanket with the second one on top of us, and we took turns of two hours each to lie awake and listen.

We were nearly caught under the blanket by the swift approach of dawn, and as we crept off the sun was already drying the night's moisture from the thick-leaved vegetation round us. There was a disused path which made movement fairly easy, and soon we were well round the back of the 4056 bump and beginning to catch first glimpses of the ridge eastward from 4392. The path which was to be our objective was visible in one undulation, and we watched it for movement while we ate our sardine and biscuit breakfast. Between us and the path an ominously steep nullah with many smaller tributaries wound its way to the plains, and the plains at last looked near enough to be real and not the mirage they had seemed from Kennedy Peak.

By 07.30 hrs. we had rounded the hill and found a place from which we could watch both the near side and back of the Japanese positions on 4392 and also a long stretch of vital path. Too long a stretch in fact, because it was quite open from the point where it first appeared over the crest above Dollouang to our left. And, worse than that, the ominous nullah began with an almost sheer drop which started right up against the crest itself. Our beautiful plan on the map had met its first big snag. Apart from the difficulty of ambushing so open a path, the only part we could reach without crossing the nullah happened to lie just forward of the Jap positions and it therefore seemed doubtful if they used it. The first thing was to find out if they did, and we settled down for a day's watch—one of us with binoculars fixed on the path, another watching for any movement from 4056 to the rear, the third one resting.

*   *   *

L/Cpl. Graham saw them first—at about three o'clock in the afternoon. They were about half a mile away across the nullah —it would have taken us another day to get any nearer—but we could plainly see seven men leading mules and we could hear the clank of the camouflaged water packals on their backs and an occasional high-pitched shout as the animals were urged along.

All the Japs were stripped to the waist and apparently not all carried arms. They disappeared, as I feared they might, into the strip of jungle which led up to the back of their positions on 4392, and re-appeared later hurrying towards the plains. Presumably they intended to get back to their base before nightfall. They were well spaced out—this would have made an ambush difficult—but they were taking no precautions. The first man, a great hulk of a fellow, was leading three mules, and he heaved them along with his eyes fixed on the ground ahead.

We waited another hour. No more Japs appeared, and the problem remained as we had guessed in the morning—at the place where we could probably get away with a prisoner there did not seem to be any Japs, while from the place where one could be caught we could not hope to bring him back. Anyway we had yet to get home, and we started off an hour before dark because I wanted to check on 4056 on the way. We had not gone far when we found the first sign of occupation—a large notice in Japanese with an arrow pointing up the hill. This was later translated to mean 'Battalion Headquarters five hundred yards this way', but as we could not read the language we merely pocketed the sign and obediently followed the arrow. Soon we crossed a brushwood fence and an outer ring of shallow foxholes, and, not without some false alarms from the usual jungle noises, we eventually penetrated a completely empty defensive position with bunkers and bashas big enough to hold several hundred men. It was in good condition, and though we found but few identifications, it was apparently only recently abandoned.

The climax came when we spotted two valuable-looking sheets of paper near the centre of the area. Covered by Whenray's Tommy gun I pounced triumphantly upon them—to find later they were printed pages torn from English books. One was entitled *Death to the Führer,* and the other *Jungle Thrillers.*

It was almost dark now. With a last look at Dollouang

village, partly to check the rumour that it was full of pineapples—it was not—we sidled back down the hill to pick up our route home, and after a few hours' rest during which we ate sardines on cheese and refilled our water-bottles we started the climb back. Just as we were beginning to hope we had got safely through we suddenly felt tired and as suddenly things went wrong.

By trying to get through the jungle without making too much noise we were forced off our guiding spur, and before we realized what had happened we were clinging to the trees to stop a headlong fall. The compass rescued us from that disaster, but after it was over we felt we needed a few hours' rest, and we travelled miles looking for one small flat resting spot. It was extraordinarily difficult to tell the level of the ground by night, and several times we tested it gingerly only to find one of us—usually me, the heaviest—tobogganing off into the dark. Another bit of unpleasantness was a steep slope —all the slopes are steep in this story!—of bush and thin bamboo. It was too wiry to cut, and too closely knit to penetrate by parting each separate branch or by crawling underneath. I got so cross that regardless of noise I said 'Jolly old jungle' or words to that effect and charged it as though ramming a stubborn door.

By later afternoon the great reconnaissance was over, and we joined the others back at base. The rest of the Platoon had arrived during our absence, and in case they had been seen I sent them off the next day to do an ostentatious patrol in an empty village away to the north and then disappear in a direction away from base area.

Meantime we weighed the choice between a definite if difficult kill and a very problematical prisoner. One suggestion was to entice out the Japs by taking a ball along and challenging them to a match on a rolled-out soccer ground we had spotted near the Inspection Bungalow at Dollouang. But actually, although pretending to be wrestling with the problem for two days and nights, I had already made up my mind that the only way to obey orders and also be sure of some action was to attempt both choices.

So I made a model of it all one morning while the N.C.O.s went forward to view the ground, and briefed the whole party on their return. I was to take one section to lay an ambush at a point on the path about a mile and a half behind 4392. Sgt. Leonard with the other two Sections was to lie up above Dollouang and try to snaffle any Jap who ventured down towards the village, and I reckoned once he and his men had revealed themselves they could make a good getaway by crashing straight back down the Pimpi track. My section would have to depend upon its wits to get clear, but we did not intend to be hampered with prisoners.

That afternoon we all practised our ambush positions, and we sorted out rations for a four days' trip. My Section consisted of Cpl. Whittaker, so far chiefly famous for his tenor voice, L/Cpl. Powell, a Somerset farmer, Pte. Robinson, who never looked strong enough to carry himself but who usually seemed to have a bigger load than anyone, Pte. Spearritt, who was one of the better types bred on Merseyside, and Pte. Bastin, one of our more belligerent stretcher-bearers. We were armed with two Tommy guns, a Bren gun and three rifles.

Taking Sgt. Leonard and Cpl. Whenray with us, we started a day before the rest. These two were to do an additional reconnaissance from 4056; the remainder, guided by L/Cpl. Graham, would follow on and meet them the following night.

Our start was not auspicious. It was drizzling hard and even though the rain had stopped by the time we reached the bottom of the first nullah we still got soaked by the moisture dripping off every bush. Furthermore and during the first hour we found a pair of Japanese chopsticks in a place which had been clear the time before, and during the night we had no sooner set foot on the gloomy path below 4056 than Whenray just missed tripping over a booby-trap—a piece of string stretched across the path and attached to a Jap grenade. Since this find was immediately followed by the discovery of a freshly-dug foxhole, my 'What are we waiting for?' to the scout ahead sounded a little spurious.

The moon which had helped us earlier now made the shadows on that beastly path deeper than ever. By plodding we reached the top of the crest and here we left Sgt. Leonard and Whenray. Soon the rest of us were once more round the back of 4056. We kept moving while the moon lasted, but when we stopped our clothes were still wet and it was like trying to sleep in a cold bath. In our trio Spearritt provided the central heating in the middle while Robinson and I spent the night plucking the edge of a blanket which was only wide enough for two and a half.

The clouds of the previous day had helped to hide us during the more dangerous part of the approach, and now that we were behind the main enemy position I felt less concerned with the Japanese than with the unknown nullah which we had to cross. In spite of this my imprecations, even if I whispered, were none the less severe when I discovered that at one halt soon after we had started all six of us were cleaning our weapons simultaneously. Good weapon training if unsound tactics at a time when we were seven thousand feet below and fifteen miles in front of our lines!

On the way down we heard voices further up the nullah, but among those steep sides sound carried a long way and whoever it was remained well hidden. The last part of the descent became a precipitous scramble down a dry waterfall, and little Robinson—carrying the Bren gun as usual—had to be lowered on rifle slings on several occasions.

Down at the bottom it was most tantalizing. The sun was beautifully warm yet we had to stay hidden in the shade. The stream was beautifully soft and cool yet we had to keep away because its noise drowned all others. The blood and bangs of war seemed futile as we quickly refilled our water-bottles in the sun-dappled stream. How very pleasant—and a good deal safer—it would have been to spend the afternoon looking up at the blue sky far above the giant trees which lined the banks!

All of a sudden Burma seemed friendly, and—I suppose because we were tired after a damp and sleepless night—it needed quite a jerk to remember the purpose behind our picnic.

The climb to the ridge was little over two thousand feet, but it took us from noon until 6.30 in the evening. The side we had to climb was serrated by many tributary nullahs, and several of these had to be crossed because the spurs leaned left-handed towards 4392. One long stretch was infested with some unbreakable creeper which must have been specially transplanted from Tokio. We would sidle carefully through an opening in the jungle only to feel a gentle tug behind, which pulled us back like elastic and in exact proportion to the strength we exerted to get clear. Another jungle joke that afternoon was a prickly fern which removed water-bottle covers and extracted bayonets from scabbards and whisked cap comforters from our heads—while we muttered through our teeth the 14th Army slogan *The Jungle is your Friend*.

So it was dark when we reached the top of the ridge and we lay in wait on the edge of the path. It was broader than I expected and obviously in regular use because the Japs with a thoroughness which they usually expended only on forward positions had dug it deeper in places and screened the sides wherever the jungle thinned.

But nobody knew whether it was used by night, and we lay quiet and watched for about three hours. If there was any traffic, so I reckoned, it would come in the early evening, and a couple of hours before midnight we moved to ambush positions in a dip in the path about half a mile from where we had settled. I was prepared to spend thirty-six hours up there if necessary, and since I wanted a day show if possible we took it in turns during the first night to do no more than listen for movement, and this merely meant lying curled up on a three-foot ledge just below the positions arranged for the morning.

I think I stayed put only because of a sharp rock which was wedged in my back, but it kept me awake all night, and I can vouch for it that 'no other Jap passed that way that night'.

For once in fact we were not beset by the usual creaks and shufflings of the jungle night, and I even went so far as to waken the surprised Spearritt by whispering in his ear a French quotation—'Entend la douce nuit qui marche'!

The word ambush probably conjures up the picture of a one-sided affair in which a gang of desperadoes have every advantage over the heroic escort of the defenceless maiden, but in our case it was not easy to find a place where we could shoot without being seen, especially when we were expecting anything from a Manchurian mule to a complete Japanese Company.

My choice was a pleasant glade coming just after a sharp rise from the plains, and I had chosen it not for its scenery but because it seemed a likely stopping-place for anyone wanting a breather. I covered the centre, and I had Robinson's Bren gun and Spearritt on my right with L/Cpl. Powell and Bastin away to the left and Whittaker down in the jungle on the other side of the path to catch the getaways.

Long hours of motionless waiting might be necessary, and since we had just had a cold and uncomfortable night we arranged to pull back out of sight one at a time to eat the inevitable sardine and relax for twenty minutes if nothing had happened by 08.00 hrs.

This was nearly disastrous. 'Adventures do occur, but never punctually', and Spearritt had hardly taken over Robinson's position on the Bren when some high-pitched Japanese voices were heard coming down the path from 4392.

In the next few interminable minutes I remember cursing myself for just having removed my bayonet for fear it was shining in the sun, feeling convinced my rifle would misfire, fearing Robinson would give the show away by reappearing before the Nips reached us, wondering the height from the ground of a Japanese stomach and what they were talking about, and envying Spearritt for having already eaten his sardine. Yet in spite of all this I did not myself fire the shot which sprang the ambush because the voices ceased suddenly and footsteps made no sound on the soft path.

After a few minutes the silence was broken by an excited squeak followed by a single shot and a burst from the Tommy guns. Our chosen spot had proved a bit too good. The Japs—there were four of them—had stopped to rest and light a cigarette. But unfortunately they had not come quite far enough, and Bastin who was end man had been spotted by the officer of the party.

Without a second's hesitation the officer drew his long curved sword, but L/Cpl. Powell winged him with a single shot before he got within cutting range. No. 2 picked up the sword as it fell and continued the attack, while 3 and 4 dived for cover down the other side of the path. There No. 3 was killed instantly by a burst from Whittaker, and I emerged to find out what was happening and saw the officer crawling across the path towards a rifle which one of his men had dropped. He was not more than fifteen yards away—luckily about my best range—and that was easy. But Bastin and No. 2 were rolling on the ground, and prodding the right one with the bayonet which had somehow got itself back on my rifle was not so easy. However, I guessed right, and No. 4 was finally finished off when movement in the long grass of his hiding place revealed the whereabouts of his dash for cover.

There was no point in waiting. There were no Japs left to tell the tale, and the shooting would have been heard back at 4392. So I gave the signal to disperse to the rendezvous after collecting identifications and the sword and scabbard as a trophy. Whittaker and I remained behind a few minutes to lay a false trail down the north side of the ridge.

All had gone well so far, though the others later complained that the stretcher bearer had had more than his share of fun. And Robinson, who had not heard the talking and had only appeared with a surprised look and a mouthful of biscuit when the shooting started, was a bit disgruntled that the Bren he had carried all those miles had not fired even one shot!

We now made our first mistake. Whittaker's jungle boots had burst, and he and I, taking an easier route down the nullah side, descended into the wrong valley. It was not worth returning to join the others because my orders had been to wait no longer than three hours at rendezvous. So we continued home on a longer route, and it was worse than longer because we had four hours' cutting through solid jungle before we dropped exhausted for the night. As a further miscalculation Whittaker and I had the packs with all the food, while the others had all the blankets! In fact, I'm still not sure which party was better off because Whittaker and I spent our first night under laurel leaves like babes-in-the-wood, our second buried beneath a bale of hay, and of these billets neither was frost-proof and the second was full of ticks.

* * *

We had doubts, too, over the fate of the others, because three times we heard small arms fire from the Dollouang direction. For ourselves, however, apart from some nasty moments when a patrol passed within feet of us and a very long and still half-hour when we were nearly stumbled on by a party of Chin villagers cutting wood for the Japs, we got back to base without trouble.

There we found the others intact, and if peace was not exactly dropping from the veils of the evening—for the Jap is a spiteful creature and might have been out chasing us—we at least had our first real sleep for five nights. Sgt. Leonard's party was intact too, but had had bad luck. First he had bumped into enemy in strength on 4056, which had previously been empty. Next his main body had sighted two patrols on the way out without being able to catch them, and finally when he did come to lay his ambush they spent twenty-four fruitless hours before returning empty-handed.

* * *

But still, four fewer Japs in the world at the price of a few cuts on Bastin's fingers was fair enough, and next day we saddled our mules and started back for Kennedy Peak feeling our fortnight had not been wasted. But on the way Dade, the Company Clerk, with his statistician's mind tabulated the casualties we had inflicted and thus calculated it would take 'B' Company another two million years to win the war.

Yet when Lord Mountbatten turned up at Kennedy Peak on the afternoon of our return—well, 'B' Company to a man felt that that was its only fitting reception.

VIII

M.S. 22

Patrols such as I have just detailed were happening to someone the whole time in the Chin Hills. Some were more productive, some less lucky; fewer, I think, gave better experience, but the main battleground continued to be M.S. 22, and until that was taken the road to the plains was blocked because the country made the supply problem too difficult to by-pass it. On the other hand the Division was not allowed at that stage of the war to risk large-scale casualties, and the result was a series of more or less painful nibbles.

'B' Company first became acquainted with these nibbles when the Battalion was in reserve to a 63 Brigade attack. This was preceded by Burma's Big Bomb for 1943—a 4,000-pounder specially diverted from the Middle East and flown over in a special Wellington. With bated breath we watched it drop as eagerly as if we expected our tickets home to burst among its fragments—and some weeks later we found the spot in the jungle where it had killed two barking deer.

The two attacking Battalions of Gurkhas crossed the start line after a twenty-minute shoot by the guns, most of the shells bursting in the trees. Here I should say the R.A.F. and R.A. both did some terrific stuff a few months later, but in those days we were only a wee speck in a world war and furthermore we were still learning that explosives dropped on a mountain pinpoint in the jungle were not as effective as in the desert.

The attack was further held up by scores of grenade booby-

O.P. WOOD
1. TRONES WOOD, N.
2. "52"

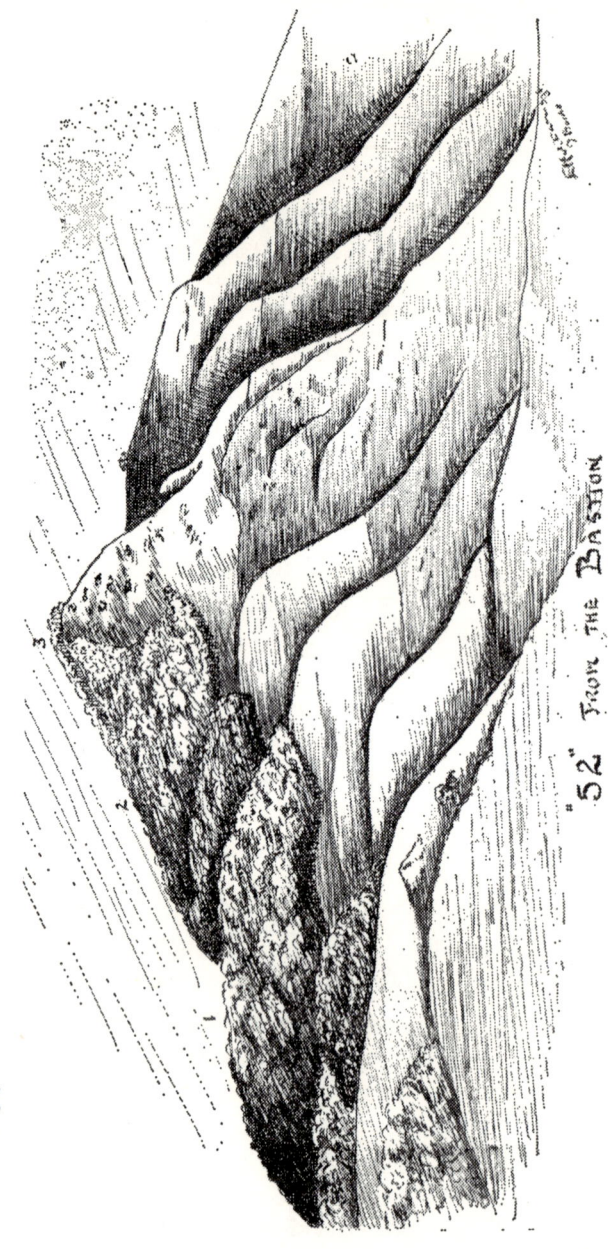

"52" FROM THE BASTION

traps which caused casualties even before the start line and left the leading troops a long way behind the barrage. However, it was nearly midday before we were called from Kennedy Peak, to find that the Gurkhas had fought their way past the snipers and foxholes which lay behind the booby-traps but had been held up along the wire in front of the main bunkers.

We set off feeling the great advance to the plains had begun, and 'Christmas in Kalewa' became the Battalion slogan. 'B' Company was leading. and our first job was to take over the defence of 63 Brigade H.Q. on the hill at M.S. 21.

The ridge was whale-backed ahead of us with a clear-cut line of jungle to the left and open downland to the right running right over the crest of M.S. 22—now only a mile away. To the right was a sheer drop to the nullah below the Thuklai ridge; to the left the jungle was very thick and almost as steep. The main ridge, like most favourite Japanese positions, narrowed considerably before the last rise to the summit and this virtually reduced any attack to a Company frontage. The road ran through the jungle about two hundred yards below this summit.

The third of the Gurkha Battalions was moving forward to continue the attack as we dug in on M.S. 21, and, apart from the occasional mortar-bomb—which proved a remarkable incentive to our digging—we were not under fire. Not from the Japs anyway, but we had not been there more than half an hour when two fighters came slipping through the clouds. 'Hurricanes, hurrah,' said the recognition experts, 'this will shake them!' And shake them it probably did, for it was *our* hill that got ten minutes most unpleasant strafing. 'I expect we've lent them the R.A.F. to make it fairer,' said Pte. Precious.

As a tribute to our digging more than to the accuracy of cannon-fire the only casualty was the Company Commander's 'charger'. This unfortunate beast, a mule-like dun pony, was just being led up the hill with the reserve ammunition when it took a shell between the legs and was last seen cantering sharply in the direction of the Japs—presumably to lodge a complaint.

This incident produced a good example of the telegraphy known as 'Road Rumour'. The next day I was asked how I enjoyed the battle, and I replied, 'Splendid, though my horse was shot from under me,' and the picture which later reached Calcutta of O.C. 'B' Company charging into battle amid a stream of shot and shell would have qualified me for a staff job with King Arthur. The rumour which equalled it went the rounds when I came back twenty-four hours late from a patrol, and the Bengal Club rang with stories of Green and I yielding at last beneath the mountainous pile of dead who had attempted to ambush us, all on the strength of one grenade burst and because I took one of my famous short cuts home.

Meanwhile the battle was going on, but by late afternoon it became obvious that M.S. 22 was not going to be taken before nightfall. Officer casualties in particular had been high. One C.O. was dead, another carried on his command from a stretcher, and in the end the Brigadier called it off and gave orders to the Battalion involved to leapfrog back to Kennedy Peak and to 'B' Company to see them all through.

Thus, a few hours after dark, the area round M.S. 21 suddenly became free of the Brigade and Battalion Headquarters which had swamped us all afternoon, and we were left amid a welter of unfinished trenches and tangled signal wire in the blackest night I remember.

Furthermore we were still responsible for our own three-inch mortars and for all the reserve ammunition of Battalion and Brigade, even though every mule and jeep had long since returned to safety. For a brief moment our wireless caught the C.O. somewhere behind us on the road, and we picked up, 'Return as ordered. We are now closing down'.

In the dark this was easier said than done, and I decided to wait till the moon rose at midnight. In the meantime all who could be spared from listening were detailed to set about burying the quantities of ammunition we could not hope to carry away. Eventually we pulled out and trailed back the six miles to Kennedy Peak carrying the mortars and water packals and several other valuables we thought the Japs did not deserve to win.

Next night I took out a string of mules and a platoon to try to recover the ammunition, and also to reconnoitre M.S. 22 for news of enemy occupation. We spent four hours unearthing our property and loading the mules without interference, and as a parting gesture we fired off the mortar bombs we could not carry. Meanwhile the patrols reported two of the main bunkers on M.S. 22 unoccupied.

It now looked as if the enemy had been more shaken than anyone thought, but all the same it was decided the Jap positions must be pinpointed before another attack was launched and that above all no new booby-traps were to be laid in front of their wire.

Our Brigade had now taken over, and for several weeks our patrols lay round and about M.S. 22 by day and by night, pulling out only when the gunners wanted to loose off a few shells in that direction. During all this time the Japs kept so surprisingly quiescent that it was difficult to tell if they were trying to bluff or if they still held the place in strength. Instead of coming out they used to try to lure us right under their guns before they opened up, and another of their little tricks was to man their fixed lines by night and then hope to attract us by clattering picks and shovels like the sounds of an innocent working party.

Their defences consisted mainly of shallow foxholes and snipers' posts which were manned only during an actual attack, and of bunkers behind two belts of wire and large enough to hold anything from two to twenty men. These bunkers were connected by four-foot crawl trenches and roofed strongly enough to withstand our shellfire, and their timber supports were beautifully finished off and fastened with iron staples. They varied in size as I have said, but one we overran later would easily have held two 25-pounders complete with

Interior of a Captured Jap. 75mm Gun Post. Feb. 1944.

gun teams. All were fitted with shelves round the machine-gun posts, and there were trenches in the floor as an escape from the bursts of any grenades we might happen to throw in.

Japanese defensive tactics were tenacious in the extreme, and not one prisoner was taken on M.S. 22. Equally brave tactics on their part broke up our two next attacks in February. The first of these overran the main line of bunkers and was consolidating on the top of the hill when it was broken up from behind by the Japs. Not enough of them had been killed off by our leading Platoon, and they re-emerged as night fell wearing British steel helmets and greatcoats and added to the general confusion by looking remarkably like Gurkhas.

Our second attack confounded tactics such as these by dropping off two men to guard the entrance of every bunker the moment it was captured, but this time the leading Company came unstuck when it swept over the top to find a false crest and three large inter-supporting bunkers firing from twenty yards' range on the reverse slope.

Our Gurkha Company had already lost over eighty officers and men in these two attacks, and with a view to saving still larger casualties a new operation called NECKLACE was planned. This set out to strangle M.S. 22 first by seizing a position on the ridge to the left—soon done brilliantly by the 1/7 Gurkhas in a night attack—and then by keeping the road under ambush by night and under shellfire by day. At the same time our left flank in the jungle was to be booby-trapped against surprise counter-attacks, and the Japs were to be kept looking strictly to their front by a Company stationed on the main ridge below them and about seven hundred yards away.

I can now bring the story back to Company level because this last job was 'B' Company's task for the two final weeks of February.

IX

OPERATION NECKLACE

There were two bits of V-shaped jungle extending across the main ridge below M.S. 22, and one—called by us Tongue Wood—lay immediately below the last steep rise to the top. The other was known as O.P. Wood, and became our base for Operation Necklace.

The perimeter of O.P. Wood which had been wired and dug by night working-parties before we entered it, sloped slightly backwards from its forward edge, and here was our observation post for the battered hill ahead. The deserted road ran just below us to our left, and our food came up daily by a jungle track just above it.

Our orders were to watch for any movement by day and to keep the Japs alert by 'Jitter Parties' at night. These were attacks aimed at drawing fire and worrying the enemy without causing casualties to ourselves, and the first half was easier to achieve than the second, because the Japs would not open up unless they fancied they were really menaced or were certain of a kill. We thus had to penetrate to their main line of bunkers every night.

A second object was to keep track of the heavy machine-guns which the Japs kept switching from bunker to bunker, and provided we made our bait sufficiently attractive we were paid the compliment of a little mortar fire or even of some shells from their 105 mm guns at Fort White—for which our counter-battery boys were always on the look out.

With four Platoons now under command (I had been lent

an extra one from 'D' Company) and both a 2-pounder and a 6-pounder gun for bunker blasting, also two 3-inch mortars together with a detachment of machine-gunners from the West Yorks and several gunner forward observation officers drawn from Medium and Mountain Batteries—to say nothing of an occasional link up with an air strike and a nightly operation to plan—it was small wonder that the troops talked about 'Supreme Company Headquarters' and that 'briefing' and 'ops' and 'communiqués' became the slang of the moment.

I had three Platoons manning the two-man bunkers built every few yards round the perimeter, and I kept a fourth for the nightly offensive and as a reserve should we be attacked. Within our small perimeter—it was oval-shaped and only two hundred yards by one hundred—everything including the so-called cookhouse had to be underground, because even if the Japs were not dropping things on us we were always liable to get the rebounding base-plates from our own 5.5 shells.

One effect of all our shelling on M.S. 22 had been to destroy most of the original jungle, and the hill was now little more than a mass of tumbled earth and fallen trees. But the main bunkers were hardly affected, except that sometimes a few openings were temporarily obscured. On the other hand, the crawl trenches were often driven in and their inhabitants thus forced to come out in the open. We thus used to see the Japs scuttling across from one hole to another whenever their front positions were being relieved or more ammunition was being sent up. One day an officer strolled the gauntlet in smart khaki uniform complete with Sam Browne and sword. This was too much even at seven hundred yards, and we built a post and two snipers manned it by day with telescopic sights on their rifles.

Competition for a twenty-minute spell in the shooting gallery was very keen. In the end we had only ten 'certainties' among our casualty claims, but there must have been many Japs who got a headache from staying underground longer than they needed for fear of the never-failing crack which would

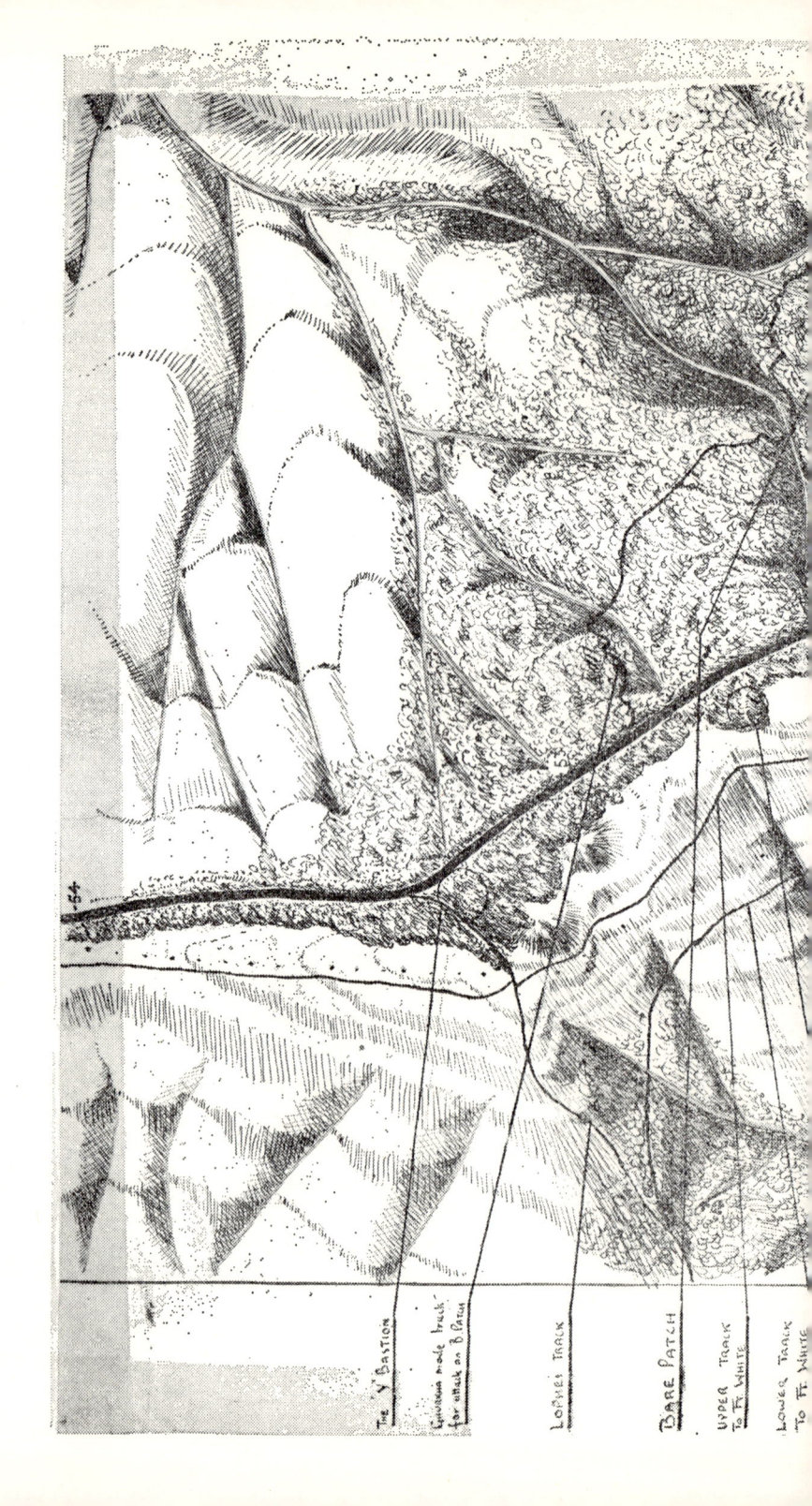

- The 'Y' Bastion
- Russian made track for attack on B Patch
- Lower Track
- Bare Patch
- Upper Track to Ft White
- Lower Track to Ft White

Reduced by one-fifth

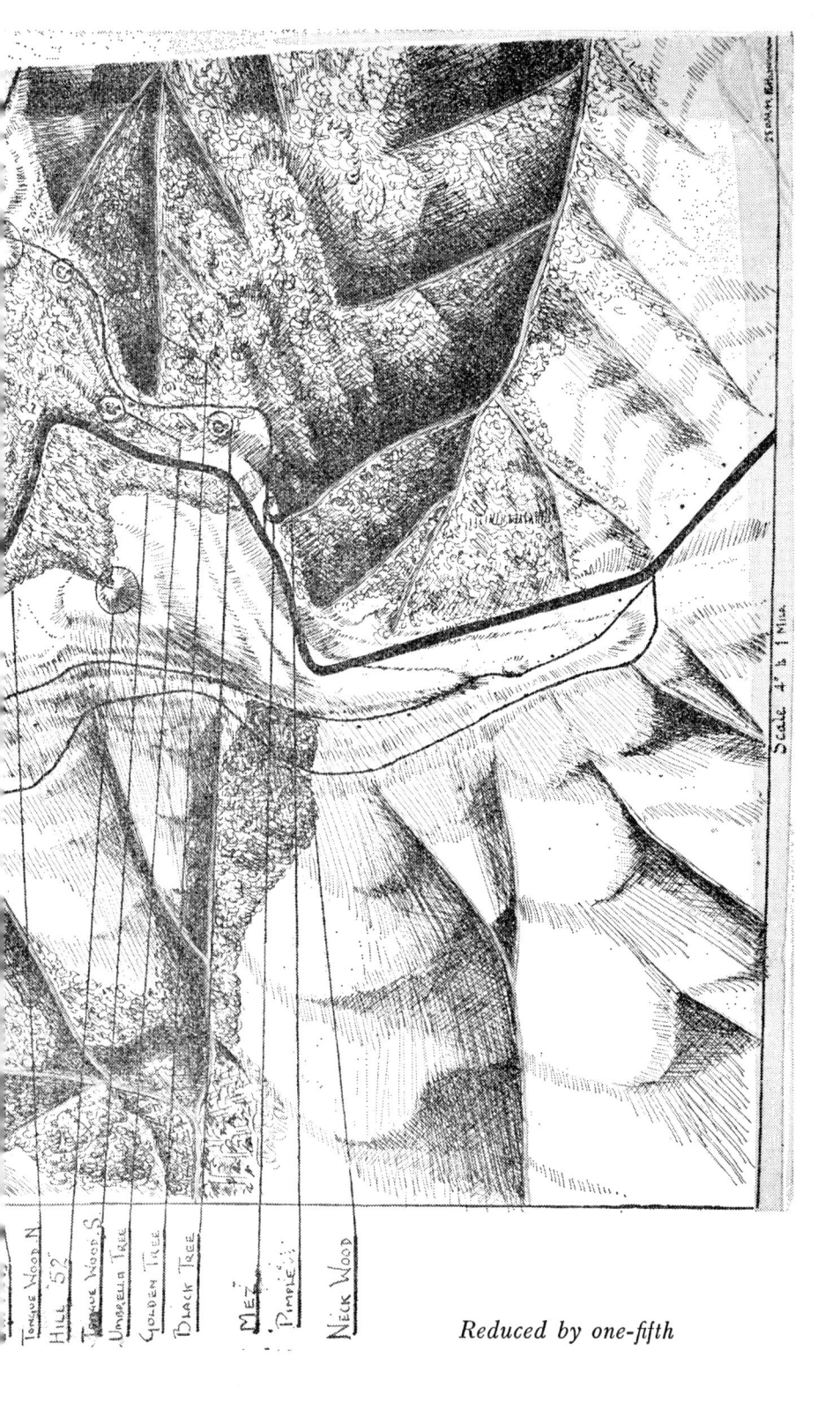

follow their emergence. On the whole, however, most of our days were quiet, and we needed rest to make up for each and every night when we were all on the alert within the perimeter or out on M.S. 22.

Each day would start with a stand-to an hour before dawn —I never knew of anyone attacking at dawn or dusk stand-to, but traditional experience has shown that these are the two best times to test alertness and check over weapons and duties. With British troops it was always difficult to stop noise in the early morning when the fifty per cent who had been off duty were getting up. 'Getting up' of course meant no more than opening our eyes and lifting ourselves off our earthy beds in the bunkers, but the ensuing noise sounded like reveille in a sanatorium for elephants with sore throats. Trying to stop the cigarette under the blanket made it better. But we never equalled the discipline of the Japs, near any of whom you could lie for hours on end without hearing sound or movement. Yet this noise of ours was not deliberate—the danger was too obvious for that. It was just that the instinctive fieldcraft of the average Briton did not match that of the enemy soldiers confronting us. But we learnt.

Fires could be lit underground—there were ways and means of dispersing smoke among the trees, and anyway the Japs knew well enough where we were. So the first performance at stand-down was the production of sundry tins of all shapes and sizes. Next came the brewing of some of our daily ration of a pint of water for a wash and a shave, and while beards were being scraped off the three Company cooks prepared breakfast. This consisted first of 'bergue', a mixture which looked like porridge but did not taste like it. It was apparently made of old leaves and chewing gum, and was followed by two slices of bread and a mug of 'char' with a couple of slices of tinned bacon and a soya link sausage and beans—or beans alone.

For tiffin we had sardines or cheese or jam and biscuits, and of course 'there was bully still for tea'. Though one night in the dark we enjoyed fresh meat—and later lamented the mule which had supplied it. Pills took the place of fresh vegetables, occasionally we had some excellent rice puddings, and on the whole we kept remarkably fit. Only a few went down with dysentery or defeated stomachs, and this was remarkable considering the distance our food had to come and the cramped life we led within half a mile of the enemy.

After breakfast the communiqué for Brigade was prepared from the accounts of those who had been out on their travels during the night, and the rest of the day was spent in cleaning weapons, checking and making up ammunition, and improving the defences generally. Before the evening stand-to at 18.00 hrs. there would always be some bumph from Battalion to answer concerning indents for lost pants or the reprehensibility of patrolling in side-whiskers.

The evening Order Group which crowded into my bunker was followed immediately by briefing for the night's 'jitters'. A jitter party might consist of any number between two and thirty men, and might be going out for anything from one hour to the whole night. Each day those of us responsible—usually myself—bent our brains to ring the change or think out some new method of attack and make our limited infantry weapons sound like those of a full Battalion. Indeed one night a heavy offensive on the flank was simulated by a single man with a bag of stones and a whistle.

*   *   *

The first of our jitter parties during that fortnight will serve as an example for the rest, though fortunately the casualties we suffered were not repeated.

I took out three Sections each consisting of four men armed with a Bren gun, a Tommy gun, and twelve grenades, and in addition I had two 2-inch mortar teams with thirty bombs apiece, and made a mobile headquarters of Sgt. Larke and three runners whose main armament consisted of a dozen Verey light cartridges. Some of these cartridges were merely for deception, the remainder were brought hopefully as being the only things we had not so far fired *at* the Japs and we were thinking that kind of smack in the eye might make a nice unpleasant change.

Zero hour was fixed for midnight, and ten minutes beforehand I came out of my bunker to check over the troops assembling silently in single file on the path above. The moon —its phases were an important factor in jungle warfare—was not due for forty minutes. We wanted to approach in the dark, and to keep contact we held on to each other's scabbards as we set off. Inside the perimeter we had already laid creeper fences to give direction, and once we were outside the wire and away from the trees the usual brilliant starlight enabled us to keep further apart. At first we moved across the west side of the ridge on open downlike grass, and in formation we were like an inverted anchor—three pairs of scouts in front, a single file in the centre, and two more pairs behind. The outside men could stop every time they felt suspicious, and whenever that happened we would all crouch down and try to pick out sound or movement on the skyline. But with each man visible only to his next-door neighbour it took considerable practice and confidence to keep control without verbal orders, and we ourselves always had to be wary not to be ambushed en route. We were always hoping to be able to catch the odd Jap engaged in his own particular branch of 'jittering'. This consisted of long-range sniping of our perimeter area with explosive bullets and sounded like an attack from the flank or rear till one got used to it, but as it helped to keep the sentries awake and no one was ever hit we did not bother much about it.

To avoid clinging to a steep hillside on the right or rustling through a very thick bit of jungle on the left there was one awkward place which always had to be passed closer than we liked on our way to the enemy bunkers. On a previous outing we discovered the Japs had it taped with a fixed line, and since it seemed the likeliest spot for an ambush I had sent out two men after dark to act as a standing patrol and give us warning.

Getting into contact with them provided the first shock of the evening. My leading scout saw a figure lying across the track on the edge of the jungle when we got near. No reply was given to the recognition signal—a low whistle—so the figure was stalked and turned out to be a headless man. Some consternation ensued until someone had the sense to use his nose as well as his eyes and realized it was a body left from some previous action. I remember several such grisly relics round M.S. 22, because while the Japs removed boots and kukries and steel helmets they never carried away any bodies but their own, in fact a few days later an N.C.O. of mine, taking cover from some premature shelling, had to choose quickly between the chance of a shell splinter in the open or the company of a rotting Gurkha in a small but otherwise secure trench.

On this particular occasion our standing patrol reported all quiet, and we left them where they were to protect the 2-inch mortar teams. Their barrage was to cover us as we pushed through the Jap wire, and it duly went off fifteen minutes later. Thanks to previous shelling, however, we did not find the wire much of an obstacle.

The next minute or two was a tricky time for any jitter party. The hillside hereabouts was so pockmarked with steep-sided shell holes that it was difficult to distinguish which was a shell hole and which was the entrance to a bunker, and until the Japs were stirred into opening fire we could not be really sure which was which. Once the shooting began—and provided we weren't in the way—we felt much happier, because the Japs always fired their automatics on fixed lines with plenty of tracer, and we thus knew more or less which areas to avoid.

One night a surprised N.C.O. heard a light machine-gun open up *underneath* him—he had stalked his way on top of a bunker without knowing it. That night, however, the chatter of an L.M.G. and the slower pop-pop-pop of a medium machine-gun broke out only a few minutes after we had announced our arrival in the area. This meant we had already done part of our job, and I breathed a quick sigh of relief at the realization that we were well and conveniently beneath the red tracer as it floated, seemingly so slowly, into the night.

The night's programme so far had merely been some blind sniping from the right and our duet of Brens from the left. A Bren in the centre and a couple of Tommy guns took on the point of origin once the Japs opened up, however, and in no time the night was filled with all the noise and fireworks of a real battle. Streams of tracer linked to form a fiery arrow pointed at the hillside, occasional ricochets bounced off the earth as if to join the stars, here and there rifles flashed and bullets whizzed into the dark as two men tried to sound like a whole Platoon.

Normally the Japs were much too used to this kind of fighting to be deceived by the greater part of our fun and games. But now they were worried enough to open up with discharge cups and mortars from behind the hill, and they even came out into their crawl trenches to lob grenades. The grenades fell harmlessly between us, the mortar bombs landed behind, the discharge cup missiles so invariably had the habit of falling in one spot that on another occasion one of my more inquiring N.C.O.s abandoned his steel helmet to test its strength and retrieved it later re-modelled by a direct hit.

It is impossible to say what casualties we caused on these excursions. A few of our luckier grenades must have penetrated through the bunker slits, and certainly we must have scored hits when the Nips came out to hurl grenades, sometimes at only twenty yards range. But either way it was the main joy of jittering that for once wasting ammunition was not a crime, and it was generally understood that a soldier returning with more than his reserve had not done his job.

* * *

We were now coming to the end of the forty-five minutes we had planned to stay, and Sgt. Larke had just begun the Verey light offensive by sinking a red into the right-hand bunker when I heard the boom of our own guns, and almost at once four shells fell right among us. The gunner officer who had come out with us to call for defensive fire if required had stayed beside the 2-inch mortar teams with orders to shoot only at my command, and for some undiscovered reason he thought we were in trouble and had taken it upon himself to let loose a salvo.

I had just left Ptes. Clarke and Louram busily firing their Bren gun with its bipod legs folded as it rested over a large shell hole. One of the shells burst so near them that as the dust cleared and the noise of whizzing shrapnel died away I—who thought I was the only lucky one to be alive—saw them calmly putting their gun on its legs because the edge of their crater had been blown away. And later that same evening I questioned Pte. Christie, whose face was covered in blood. 'No,' he replied as he lifted his hand to his cheek, 'I don't think I've been hit, sir. But my chin strap was blown right off.'

I soon discovered two of our casualties could not walk, so I gave one Section the job of carrying them, detailed the second Section to act as escort, and ordered the third to continue firing to keep the Japs from realizing what had happened.

It was not easy getting the wounded away across the craters or over the tangle of the shattered jungle, but worse followed. As soon as I had seen the carrying Section into the comparative safety of Tongue Wood I went back for the last Section and found it still stoutly making its remaining few rounds sound as impressive as possible but received the report that its corporal had not been seen since the shelling.

With a runner I searched for ten minutes—during which the risen moon seemed to shine on us like a spotlight and every stone and broken root in the undergrowth looked like a body.

We found him in the end, knocked unconscious by blast and lying under a fallen tree. He was a big fellow too. Five men—three of whom were carrying an unconscious sixth—was not the safest of parties to linger long within a few yards of a strong Japanese position. But Sgt. Larke—who always contrived to be the last in on any show—was one of the five, and we pulled slowly back hoping against hope the Japs still had their heads far enough below ground to prevent them from appreciating that two final grenades and a few defiant spits from Clarke's Bren gun represented our departure and farewell.

Back within the perimeter the cooks had wisely seized the excuse for a special brew of tea. The wounded had already been dressed, jeeps had been summoned up by wireless to meet our stretcher-bearers a mile and a half down the road to take the casualties back to Tiddim. A twenty-one mile jeep ride lay in front of them before hospital was reached.

* * *

During the fortnight we lived in O.P. Wood on Operation Necklace every man spent three if not four nights out, and thus received first-class training both in night work and ingenuity in the use of weapons and also in the experience of being under fire at close range yet master of the situation. Every one of us finished up by understanding that by hard work and a little common sense we could hardly fail to thrash the Jap at this war game he had started. But at the same time we realized how lucky we had been when by sheer bad luck 'A' Company lost two of their best N.C.O.s the second night after they relieved us.

X

DOWN THE ROAD

M.S. 22 was not taken by us, but the hill which had cost us so much trouble and so many lives fell without a fight during a much later stage of the campaign. Even by the middle of March the grip in which it was slowly being throttled had tightened so appreciably that it became obvious the Japanese must soon attack in force—or yield. Three Companies of the 2/5th were entrenched on the spurs round its eastern slopes, and we who lay on the north, west, and south-west had already made two attempts by night to wire up the southern gap.

Suddenly the reason for the Japs' quiescence became apparent. Our particular enemy, 33 Division, leaving a containing force on M.S. 22, had slipped across the Manipur river to our west and was reported to be approaching the road behind us, and at the same time two more Jap Divisions crossed the Chindwin east of Imphal. In jungle country and with our Division nearly two hundred miles in front of its base it was impossible to guard against this sort of thing happening, but it did not need Tokio's repeated radio announcements that the march on Delhi had begun to make our Corps Commander realize a considerable threat was developing both against Imphal and against our one land road to India.

17 Division was therefore ordered back, and we ourselves, having left behind a Platoon of the 2/5th to light fires and make noises so as to keep the Japs on M.S. 22 amused for an extra day, began our walk to Imphal.

Now that the whole campaign can be reviewed it seems

reasonable to have sacrificed the relatively unimportant Chin Hills in order to strengthen our position in more vital areas. The operation order for such a scheme had in fact been ready for a long time, but no one thought it would ever be needed. So many of our supplies were already being dropped by air that the idea of being surrounded caused no despair, and the Chin Hills had so long been the playground over which 17 Division had sweated and died that blood and sweat seemed the foundation from which to go forward—not back.

But war is a wasteful thing, and back we had to go. We marched out with our usual kit plus a blanket to every two men and some extra clothing in a side pack, and for some obscure reason the mosquito nets which had just been issued to us. The Battalion had its normal jeeps and mules and one 15-cwt. truck for extras, but 'B' Company's sole extra was its faithful gramophone. No extras were official, but it was amazing how easily so many had found their way to us up The Road. And now all these joined blankets and greatcoats, and quantities of food, in a magnificent orgy of destruction.

Orders to move had come at dawn on March 13th, and by sunset both Brigades were under way. We ourselves marched off into the night as the road behind us was blown down the khud side and while our stores and buildings at Tiddim were going up in smoke and flames.

In the Company little was known of the main situation, and the chief thought among the Sections and Platoons weaving off into the general line was of covering the forty miles which lay behind us and the sunrise. We knew the Japs were somewhere on our flanks, but the whole vast pattern of the forces now moving into battle meant far less to us than the strong rumour that transport would meet us at M.S. 126. The battle for the frontiers of India and the news that the Japanese forces had been told by General Mitaguchi, 'the success of this invasion will have a profound effect on the course of the War, and may even lead to its conclusion', seemed far less important than the worry as to whether the soles would this time last on

Pte. Partridge's boots, or whether Pte. Ditchburn had destroyed and not swallowed the rum supply we had to leave behind.

Dawn found us well beyond the foot of the 'chocolate staircase', and the air was full of rumours of the overwhelming of the West Yorks' flank Platoons as they pulled out from the hills above. This was true, but whether or not the Japs shared in the battle which took place the next night is a matter of considerable doubt.

'B' Company, on the far side of the river from the main body and knowing less about the cause than most, heard this battle start. Somewhere, something had moved in the darkness, possibly Japs but certainly no more than a patrol. Someone, making a challenge which was not answered, fired into the night. Eyes strained by the effort and uncertainty of the last few days saw crawling enemy figures in every bush, and fingers which should have known better squeezed easy triggers—at nothing. All this was a reaction of nerves which would seem impossible in experienced troops, but Gurkhas who had been in action right across Burma for the past two years started pouring away precious ammunition as fast as British troops, faster even than Indians of the Mountain Regiment who had never seen a Jap. In the morning it all seemed very stupid, except for the unfortunate casualties—and the Divisional Commander's rude remarks.

* * *

A few more miles, and the first real action developed when some jeeps of 63 Brigade ran into an ambush at the point where the road climbed over the hills before dropping down to the Manipur river at M.S. 126. The guns deployed quickly —if staggering one gun behind another along our one and only road can be so described, and the Gurkhas went storming into action. It was soon over, and the Division lumbered forward once again with our Brigade now taking the lead.

At M.S. 126 the road had been broadened and a new bridge recently built to take three-ton lorries. Here we expected trouble—our transport too—but we all got across safely and blew the bridge behind us. Then we found the Japs entrenched on the hills on the far side, and the fight which followed was to repeat itself with varying severity all the way to Imphal.

The Japs holding the hills above, put up a road block and covered it with fire. We located them with infantry patrols, sent a Battalion on a long chukker round on the flank, deployed the guns, whistled up the R.A.F. from Imphal, and in due time reopened the road after having killed as many of the enemy as possible.

As the leading infantry we spent most of our time surmounting all the different types of country which lay parallel with the road on either flank and varied in texture from the thick jungle by the river bottoms through intervening stages of scrub-covered slopes and trees to bare rugged hillsides where visibility suddenly became extreme and every bullet ricocheted off in a little puff of dust. This was tough country, and one night we marched for hours through wet grass so thick and high above our heads that we felt we must break out or suffocate. The Japs of course knew where we were and what was happening as soon as they saw the flames of Tiddim, and gloated daily on their wireless that 17 Division was in the bag at last.

Two things alone prevented this from coming true. First air superiority, without which no guns or jeeps or ambulances, bound as they were to one single road, could possibly have got through. Secondly the fortunate fact that the Japs, forced to use jungle tracks for their lines of communication, could never get their supplies up fast enough to make a road block sufficiently solid to stop us before we burst it open. They followed us very quickly down the road and over the bridges—every one of which we blew behind us—and soon they had light tanks on our tail. But their main forces were always in front, trying in vain to annihilate us before we could reach Imphal.

Perhaps if by leaving Tiddim even one day later we had given them a little more time, they might have succeeded. . . .

In our little action at M.S. 126 the Japs were cleared with the help of Bofors guns firing accurately over open sights into their bunkers. Nevertheless we temporarily lost part of the area, and a gunner officer had the unpleasant experience of being tied to a tree by the Japs and subjected to thirty minutes of British shelling before our counter-attack released him.

The next appreciable battle was in and near M.S. 109. By now this valley below the steep hills from which we had been plucked so hurriedly some five months earlier had been turned into a Q supply depot of engineer and ordnance stores, and there was also a hospital and a transit camp and large dumps of clothing and canteen goods. The Japs, whose operation order stressed the need for the capture of just such a place, had captured it four days before we arrived after a short fight with the 'soft' troops who manned it but who had been able to hold on long enough for all the stretcher cases to be cleared from the hospital. This was fortunate, because the usual Jap treatment for overrun wounded was a quick thrust with the bayonet.

'B' Company were scattered in Platoon picquets on various mountain tops when 'C' and 'D' Companies went into the first attack. It did not succeed, and was chiefly memorable as the cause for the translation of our C.O. to a higher sphere, and one in which he could do less damage. 'Don't bother about maps, the enemy are on one of those hills over there, "X" Company will bum along this ridge and capture their position, the Brigadier mentioned guns in support, ask the Adjutant about zero hour. I saw a "B" Company man looking tired yesterday, "B" Company will dig the latrines on consolidation. Why isn't any tea ready?' was his method of giving orders, and our Second-in-Command took his place amid general rejoicing.

The position was finally won back by the 2/5th Gurkhas after a magnificent attack in which the shooting did not seem to stop for hours, and the other occurrences of note that day were the death of two unfortunate Indians who, getting too near the supply-dropping area, were hit on the head by bully beef tins, and the delivery of a wounded elephant lately used by the Japs for the transport of their 75 mm guns. It was secured by the Medical Officer who promptly transferred it to the Quartermaster.

M.S. 109 had been freely looted. Bits of clothing and tins of food littered the paths for miles around, but there was still enough left for us to have several good meals and change our tattered clothing for new shirts and trousers and boots. An odd result of this was to be seen in a Company fight a few days later when both ourselves and the Japs appeared in identical clothes.

* * *

M.S. 109 was no exception to the inflexible army rule that Army stores must be kept full, however pathetically worded the indents of Company Commanders further forward, and after re-equipping our mules with harness and our jeeps with spare wheels and our weapons with spare parts—all of which the depot wallahs had kept as successfully hidden from the Japs as from ourselves—we destroyed such stores and transport as could not be carried away with us, and then departed.

Meanwhile a Brigade of 23 Division, coming along the road to meet us, had cleared one road block with the aid of light tanks from 7 Cavalry. From our side of M.S. 109 I was ordered to send a patrol to make contact, and Sgt. Irving completed the link-up by night but came back with the news that the Japs had again appeared on the road at M.S. 82.

Clearing this was a 'B' Company battle in the best Battle Drill style. We advanced to contact almost in single file, the leading Section of 10 Platoon was pinned by cross-fire, the other two Sections swept to a flank to take the first knoll. Then, supported by their fire, the two remaining Platoons flanked again to finish off the Japs who stayed behind and to eat the rice and pork hospitably left cooking. Easy when it works, and we added Vanglai to the rising sun on our Company battle honours flag.

This time our transport really was meeting us at M.S. 72—so it was said—and before the road was finally clear we reached country flat enough for us to be able to construct the two hundred yard airstrip from which our baby aeroplane could land and fly off with the wounded who had bumped so uncomplainingly down the road with us for nearly three weeks. A rare enemy aircraft appeared just as one of these defenceless Austers was taking off, I remember. Like a sparrow from a hawk the Auster flew up the nearest nullah. The Zero in pursuit, unable to fly slowly enough, had to zoom up to avoid hitting the steep hillside, and when it returned to the attack the Auster, literally hiding behind the trees, got clean away without a shot being fired.

Our ambulances—followed during the next few days by our Battalions—were escorted into Imphal on the very night the Japanese radio announced that their crack 33rd Division had completed the slaughter of the 'cowardly Black Cats', and 'of 17 Division only the Commander and twenty-six men lived to tell the tale'.

Ninety per cent of the two thousand vehicles and four thousand mules which had left Tiddim three weeks earlier won through to the Imphal plain. Transport had met us at last at M.S. 32—and this meant we would have walked a mere one hundred and fifty miles had we kept strictly to the road. We were tired, and we could have done with a series of large and peaceful meals. But at no time had anyone been really short of food, and the twenty-six men claimed by the Japs as the sole survivors of a Division ten thousand strong were to be found in any one of our Platoons.

'B' Company had the fantastically light casualty list of eight wounded as the net result of three weeks' fighting in a 'doomed Division'. Sgt. Little and Pte. Hind had been killed while serving with other Companies, but the total in killed, wounded, and sick in the whole Battalion did not exceed one hundred. All those who needed hospital treatment were straightway flown out to India, and the rest of us joined the garrison of the fortress. The siege of Imphal had already begun.

17 (Light) Indian Division badge

XI

SIEGE OF IMPHAL

The Japanese plan unfolded itself rapidly, for its soldiers were so lightly equipped that its success must depend upon speed. They needed the rich plain of Imphal and the stores we had accumulated there—and they needed both before the monsoon broke in May.

Imphal itself, the capital of Manipur State and a pleasant open town in green paddy-field country, was surrounded by low hills averaging about two thousand feet in height. There was a big all-weather air strip on the Kohima road, and another twenty miles out at Palel on the Tamu road.

The Japanese 33 Division, which had been given the task of finishing us off, lay licking its wounds on M.S. 32 on the Tiddim road, and our encirclement was completed by their 15 and 31 Divisions. They reached to just beyond Palel on the south-east to Kanglatonbi—where they had overrun another stores dump—fifteen miles north on the Kohima road, and on the jungle tracks to the east they were only eight miles away. Kohima itself was already surrounded, so no help could come by road. The barbarian conquest which had already engulfed so much of Asia had raised its flag on the soil of India, and these yellow faces which looked down from the fringe of hills round Imphal must have seen at least as far as Calcutta and Bombay and who knows what beyond? We must have seemed a very small obstacle to be standing in the way of so glittering a prize.

Lord Louis Mountbatten dropped unexpectedly out of the

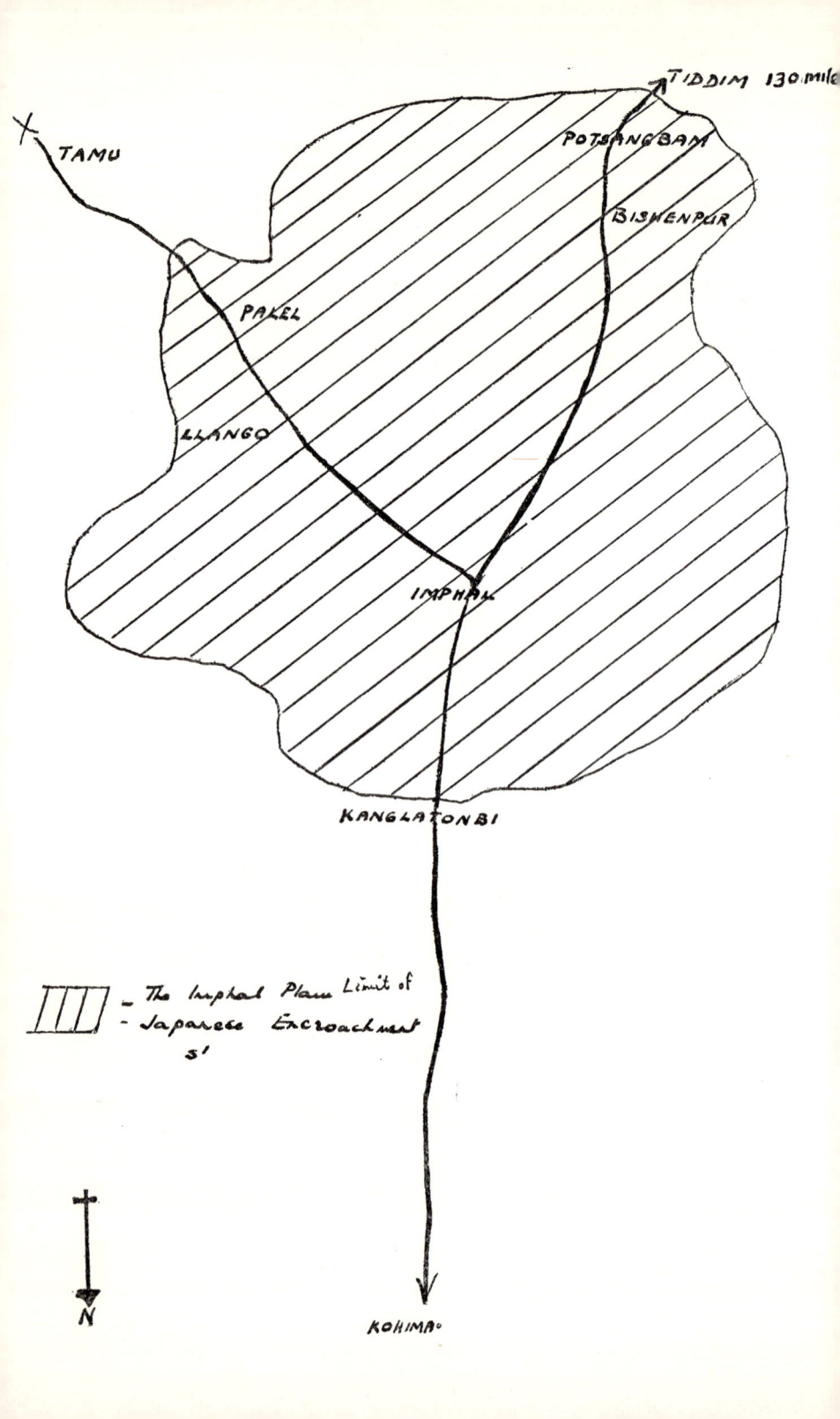

TIDDIM 130 mile
POTSANGBAM
BISHENPUR
TAMU
PAKEL
LLANGO
IMPHAL
KANGLATONBI

▭ = The Imphal Plain Limit of
- Japanese Encroachments

N

KOHIMA

skies a few days after we arrived, assembled all available troops round him, and told the exact nature of the threat. To meet it, he said, a fourth Division was to be flown in complete from the Arakan and aeroplanes were being sent from the Middle East to fight for us and diverted from the China 'hump' to supply us.

So our frontier skirmishing had suddenly become part of the big War, and after that talk we felt better than we had done for weeks. One big advantage which resulted from the type of fighting in which the Division had been engaged was that we had all got to know each other far more intimately than is usually the case. The Corps Commander, General Scoones, whose Headquarters had once been a hundred and sixty-four miles from Tiddim, was familiar to us by now, and often stopped to talk with the Company; officers and men of Gurkha and British Battalions had acquired a camaraderie which was consummated in the work we had done together and had been finally cemented by our three weeks' struggle down The Road.

Back in Imphal we were given a rest area of hills and lakes on the Tamu road, but we only spent one morning there, and after absorbing some reinforcements which were awaiting us we just managed to find time to dig yet another series of unused defences. During the afternoon while on Church Parade —it was Easter Sunday—we were ordered to hasten in support of 63 Brigade in the Kanglatonbi area.

There we formed a defensive box with a Battalion of an airborne Brigade which had come to Imphal for a little quiet training and had promptly found itself surrounded by Japanese. They were reorganizing too, and by good fortune nearly a fortnight passed without either of us being involved in action. Not that we were idle. We had to patrol some very wild country to the west where the Japs had just cut the track to Silchar and were boasting that 'the last escape route of the trapped 4th Corps had now been blocked'.

There was no need for such boasts. We had no intention of

escaping, and all we wanted was a wash and no war for a few days. On the east the Japs had already penetrated to a hill about six miles away from which their guns could shell our main air strip; and they must have found it difficult to reconcile Tokio's insistence on our desperate efforts to escape with such of our activities as they could see through their glasses. These included swimming in the river, and playing Company games of Rugby football.

During this time there were a few air raids, but I remember no other excitement than some indiscriminate night shooting which started another attack of 'jitters' and finished in an undignified scrap between the 3rd Dragoon Guards and a Mobile Bakery which had acquired some machine guns.

Meanwhile the Kanglatonbi threat had been beaten off by 63 Brigade, but a more serious situation had developed on the Tamu road where the Japs had been raiding the air strip at Palel from the long spur which overlooked it and which they had recently seized.

On May 6 our Brigade assembled for the battle which was to follow two nights later, and we had done so many attacks in which there had been no time for detailed orders and in which unknown ground dictated the course of the battle that on this occasion it was a treat to have time for organization.

From our assembly area we could see the ridge on which our objective—the village of Llango—lay, some ten miles away. On the left the ridge rose to Woody Peak, a height of over three thousand feet. We were to attack from the far side, however, and it was typical of the fighting in this kind of country that Company Commanders should be able to receive their orders from the back of the enemy's position.

When I returned from the pow-wow I made an earth model on which every man saw the whole plan, and in that respect it was almost like early days in England when the Company Commander signed the nightly and irrevocable detail for next day's parades. This was to be a night attack after a silent approach march, two Battalions attacking and one forming a

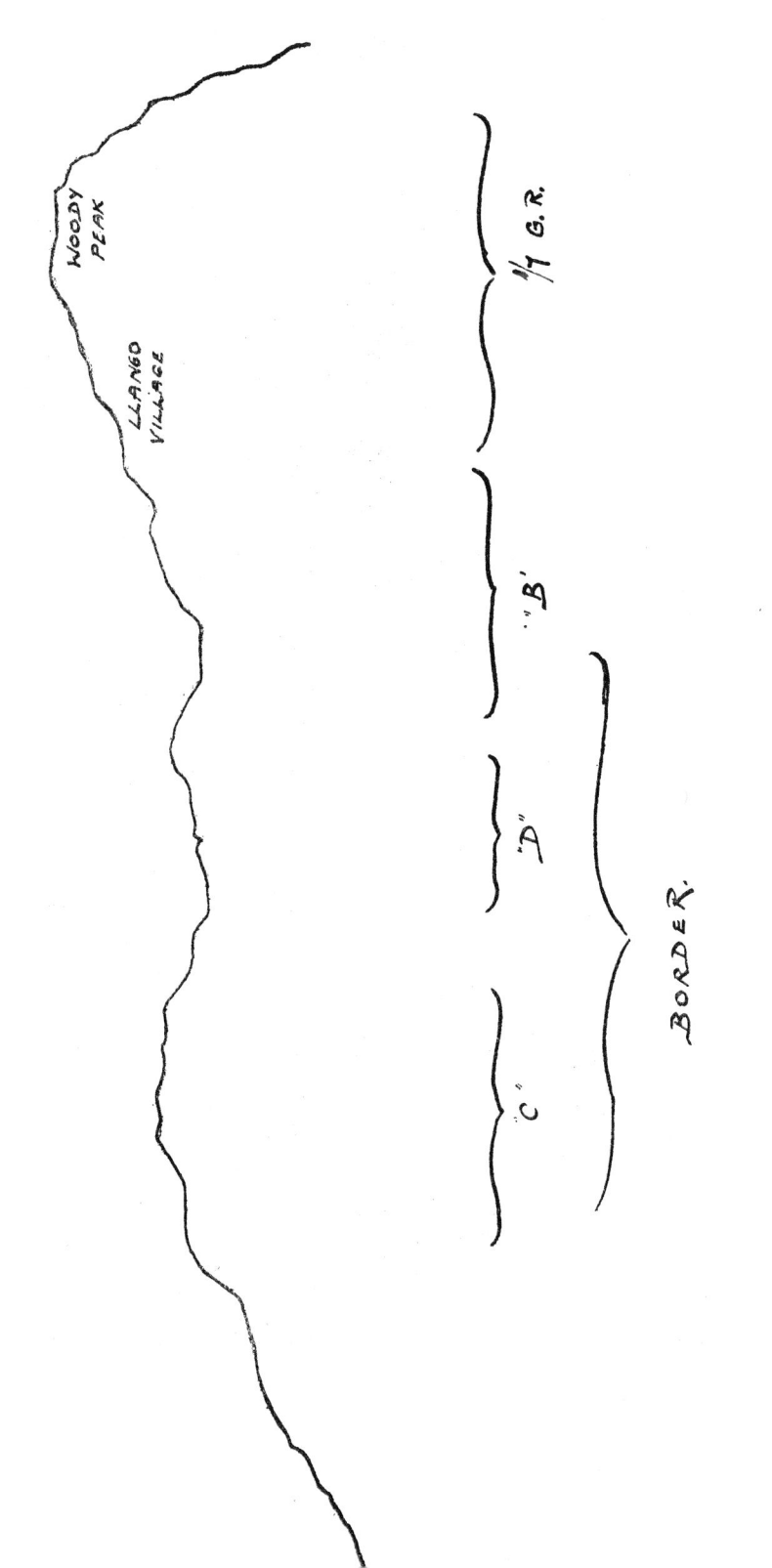

WOODY PEAK

LLANGO VILLAGE

1/7 G.R.

"B"

"D"

"C"

BORDER.

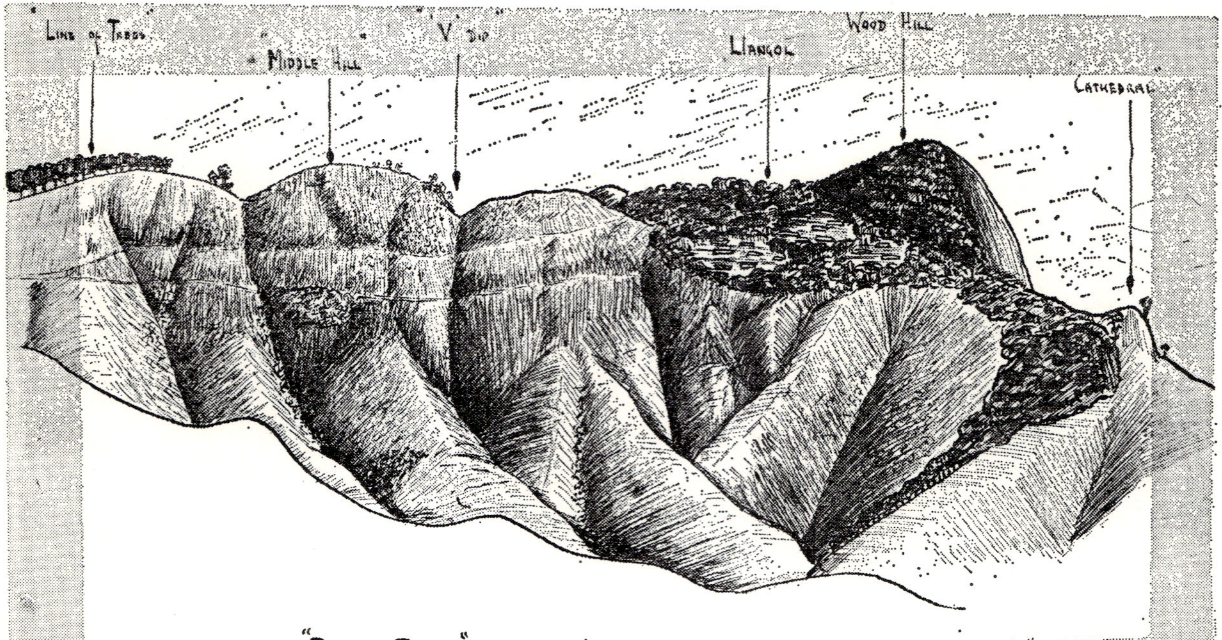

"BLACK RIDGE" — LLANGOL. MAY 6th 1944.

Sgt. Int. Section
9 Border.
Del 14th 1944.

block on the Japs' escape route. Some tanks were in reserve in case things went wrong, and the guns and R.A.F. were to be used only after the Japs started to run away.

The thought of Japs running seemed a bit optimistic to us, but after all they were not our old enemies of the Chin Hills. This time we were to meet 15 Division and they might have different views on what their Emperor expected of them. Another incentive from our point of view was the intelligence that their General was firmly supposed to have six concubines attached to his headquarters, and the hope that we might catch him with his defences down added interest to the chase.

On the other hand the carefully-worded orders covering everything from Orientation to Intercommunication, together with the sense of planning implied in an operation which looked as far ahead as 'D Day plus two', and the unusual fact that the C.O. even found time to answer the doctor's usual irrelevant questions, led to the unreal feeling of being once again on a tactical course at the training school. We had, too, memories of certain past misunderstandings which had occurred on Company training by night—yet this was to be a Brigade attack with the Battalion going in without a moon and three Companies up. . . .

Woody Peak and Llango village, the objectives of the 1/7th, lay on the right as viewed from the direction from which we were launching our attack; 'B' Company's objective was from the edge of the village to a wooded dip some five hundred yards to its left, 'D' Company were to go for a hill on our left again, 'C' Company had to seize the bare peak which lay beyond it, and 'A' Company were in reserve.

We reached the assembly area just before dark, ate several enormous dixies of stew, and tried to get a little sleep before we set off. Companies were to leave at half-hour intervals, and while the first part of the route was to be in every case the same, the final approach had to be by separate spurs. Zero hour for the actual attack was fixed at ten minutes to four in the morning. 'B' Company led off at ten o'clock at night; this

I reckoned would give us an hour to spare if the route was difficult, and at any rate time for a breather on the start line.

Hints of all this detailed planning have probably led to the expectation of a major disaster, but it was not to be so. For once a complete Brigade operation at night was to go 'according to plan' yet how many petty and individual troubles those three words may hide, and I remember a few during the five minutes while we were assembling to move off.

Waiting in the dark for reports to reach me that all were ready, I was approached by a man who blurted out in a hurried whisper that by that morning's mail his wife had asked for a divorce. 'I'll talk to you about it in the morning' seemed an inept reply to a man in his frame of mind with five hundred Japs between him and the sunrise. Then Dade, my Company Clerk, fell and broke his glasses, and that meant a runner had to take over the portable 'office', a side pack containing signal pads for messages, code names, chinagraph pencils, and other odds and ends of battle which Dade knew I might suddenly demand.

Next a man limped up with an ankle he had just strained. If genuine and I took him, he might have to fall out and be lost; if I left him behind, his Section was short of a lot of ammunition. I could only take a chance on my knowledge of his character and distribute his Bren magazine and grenades among men already carrying top weight. Usually the man who fell out was discovered later to be carrying the Section's bully beef or his Platoon's tea ration for several days, but luckily on this occasion we were carrying American 'K' rations and everyone had their own.

One of the things we had really learned during our Bengal training was how to move by night in single file. In jungle country it was often the only way and may not sound difficult, but just try it with a hundred men! Speed was hard to regulate with obstacles to climb over or through, and gaps would occur. Suddenly a man, realizing that Private Soap in front of him had disappeared, would say to himself 'Oh, well, I'm bound to catch him up in a minute', and half an hour later the Company would be in two halves a mile apart. The only way was for the man in front to stop the moment he discovered a gap had occurred, and this needed signal taps on the shoulder to begin with, but after a while became instinctive. In the same way, we learned after crossing any serious obstacle to wait for a signal from the back before restarting.

The split on our approach to the Llango battle was entirely my own fault. We had had a difficult walk up a dry stream bed and through a thick bit of jungle before climbing the last spur which led to the ridge. 10 Platoon and Company Headquarters were all right. But the others, I knew, were beginning to straggle, and instead of waiting I left the C.S.M. and a runner with instructions to bring on the stragglers to the ridge straight ahead and outlined against the sky. There we could rest better, I thought, and I could check our position. But ten minutes later the ridge was covered in mist and straight ahead meant nothing.

A lucky patrol and our bird call recognition signal found the rest, but not before it seemed I was going to be compelled to put in a Company attack with one Platoon. And by this time our reserve of time had almost been used up, and matters were not made any easier when we were nearly ambushed by a Company of Gurkhas who had strayed from their route.

For the sake of secrecy the last part of our route had not been reconnoitred, and though we were able to find our landmarks with the help of a compass the climb itself turned out to be practically vertical. Fearing every minute a Bren gun would go clattering away, we hauled ourselves up hand over fist with only a single Section in front to screen us, and after a march of five and a half hours in the dark we reached the path laid down as our start line five bare minutes before zero hour.

These five minutes ticked away slowly as pins were loosened in grenades and bayonets clicked gently on rifles. It seemed strange to have no barrage as our overture, and in the silence one could sense the lines of men clinging to the black hillside —a hillside hardly a dozen Britishers had trodden before and now about to spit death at men who had never expected to travel beyond their Lakeland fells. What futility drove us on? Why not shout to the Japanese Commander, 'You're going to lose Burma and the War in the end, so don't imagine shooting a few of us can stop it! Let's all let each other live tonight and talk it over in tomorrow's sun.'

It was now 03.50 hrs, and talking was definitely off, and 10 Platoon on the right with 11 Platoon on the left had moved off to contact. It was all to the good that so far the Japs had caught none of us before the start lines, and the spurs which held the Gurkhas and our other Companies away to the right and left were as still and eerie as our own. Flames were crackling somewhere behind the hills, however. Probably the thatched roof of some village house had caught a spark from an open fire, and maybe the Japs were busy putting it out. Or was it a trap? Were those hills so empty after all?

And then the party started.

First the unmistakable slow stutter of a Jap medium machine-gun followed by two quick 'whoomphs' which I hoped were our own grenades. Almost immediately a rain of mortar bombs burst as brightly and harmlessly as fireworks and about two hundred yards ahead, and through it all I heard the opening crackle of 11 Platoon's Brens. 'Johnny-get-your gun, Johnny-get-your-gun . . .' they said. Four shots a burst, and steady shooting. They must have found a target somewhere in the dark, and the story soon came back with the Platoon runner. He was a very cross man. A Jap had just called out to him, 'Send me the Platoon runner,' and he was angry not because he had almost forgotten we had a recognition signal laid on in case of just such a trick but because 'the little yellow basket had the nerve to talk to me in English, sir!'

The events represented by the bangs already described were soon explained—11 Platoon's leading Section had surprised both themselves and the Japs by getting within ten yards of a machine-gun before it opened fire. The leading Section dropped a couple of grenades on it and pulled back a bit to reorganize while the rest of the Platoon attacked. In the meantime mortar bombs kept bursting further down the hill as though the Japs were firing on S.O.S. lines chosen in anticipation of our attack coming from the opposite direction.

Away to our left there was considerable shooting and shouting from 'D' Company's objective, and the 1/7th had started to fight on Woody Peak. You could always recognize the Gurkhas in action because there never seemed to be a pause; somebody was always shooting, and it was heartening now to hear the crackle on our right flank, like the constant rattling of a dozen dice boxes. By now 10 Platoon were in the battle too, but sent word to say they had reached the top of the hill and that all was well. So I committed Sgt. Larke with 12 Platoon, all of whom had been pawing the ground behind me.

In an hour's time the hill was ours. The mist came down again before the end and some Japs got away, but they had left behind all their food and equipment—including three large flags, and a lot of mines—and for once we had made them run.

We whizzed off our success signal on the Verey pistol, and we were digging in hard by the time the dawn had warmed away the scarves of mist which still wreathed the jungle trees. In what was left of Llango village we linked up with the Gurkhas still clearing snipers from Woody Peak, and we heard by wireless that 'C' Company had been almost unopposed. Only 'D' Company's hill in the Battalion centre still held out in strength.

I took a Platoon to help in the attack which cleared it, and this attack was notable only for the fact that after over six months' fighting we took our first Japanese prisoner. Needless to say he was wounded in both legs!

Back with the Company, where the digging was almost

finished, we just escaped paying dearly for a bad mistake. The hill was still being searched with Jap mortar fire, and Harrison, a signaller, had been hit rather badly in the back. Company Headquarters gathered round to a man—like staring moonies at a street accident—and another bomb fell slap through the trees above our heads! A hurried if belated scatter took place before we realized it was a dud, and we watched it roll innocently down past Green, and down the hill. For a Company Commander and his complete Headquarters to have been written off by one small bomb would not have been popular, especially when the Company Commander had spent so much of his Army life uttering the well-worn words, 'Don't bunch'.

In the meantime Harrison, who had been ruefully claiming a stretcher, confessed after the scatter that he must now consider himself as 'walking wounded'.

Soon after 10.00 hrs the bugle call which represented the Battalion success signal announced that the whole ridge was ours. So 'Char-brewing' could now commence.

* * *

'B' Company took over Woody Peak that afternoon and had the pleasure of listening to the Japs running into the 2/5th's block across their escape route. Our mules were soon up with tools and reserve ammunition, and during the two days before we were relieved by a Patiala Battalion there were sundry scares but no real troubles except lack of water and the burying of many pieces of Jap.

Over three hundred of them had been killed in that attack, and 'B' Company's casualties consisted of one killed and eight wounded—including Arnold Schlund who sprained his knee. 10 Platoon said it happened while he was leading their attack, but his brother officers swore the accident occurred when he heard there was a rum issue.

XII

THE ROAD AGAIN

Back in an assembly area after the Llango show my chief memory is of the enormous meal awaiting us the night we came in. Gavin Elliot was now Second-in-Command of the Battalion and as such not allowed to do any fighting, and instead he had raided the larders for miles around. Fortified by curry from the Gurkhas and bacon from the Seaforths and tinned fruit from the R.A.F. and chickens from the Manipuri, we went to sleep thinking how nice it was to fight a Jap Division which sometimes made mistakes and had the sense to realize when it was beaten.

But our sleep of repletion was cut short, because at six o'clock next morning we received orders to move back to the Tiddim road where our old enemies had spilled out of the hills and now held the road at the thick bamboo village of Potsangbam. They had been attacked by tanks and blasted from the air, but by keeping themselves supplied at night they had so far proved impossible to dislodge. Moreover, Potsangbam—soon of course to be known as 'Pots and Pans'—held the key to a line of hills parallel to the road along which Jap raiding parties were penetrating far up the road towards Imphal.

Ours was not to be a defensive role. 63 Brigade with ourselves under command was to attack up the road. The other two Battalions of our Brigade were going far round to the left to form a block behind, and between us 33 Division was to be finally destroyed.

We had two nights en route, and these again were memorable mostly for their food. In the Company area six fat pigs lived and a field of spring onions grew. We twice had fresh meat and vegetables—the first for many weeks—before an official ban was put on further killings. I happened to be with the C.O. a few hours later when a rattle of shots sounded from my Company area, and the telephone was seized, and 'B' Company asked in no sweet terms if once again they were disobeying orders and shooting pigs. 'Oh no, sir,' came the sad reply. 'It's only the Japanese.'

That night we moved further up the road to a village named Kwa Sipahi, about a mile from 'Pots'. All these villages were made of mud-walled houses, built under the shade of bamboo and banana palms. Like oases they stood on the flat plain, upon which the locals kept their cattle in dry weather or cultivated rice in wet, but between each cluster of houses with their thick bamboo-fenced gardens ran paths flanked by ditches which were often deep and wide enough to stop a tank.

For months the theory had been 'If only we could entice the Japs out on the plains we would soon have them on the run'. Well, now they were on the plains, but we couldn't get at them. Tanks which avoided Jap anti-tank guns would either bury their noses in the ditches or fail to penetrate the walls of wiry bamboo. Infantry would get hold of a village edge by night, only to be slaughtered by fire from hidden bunkers by day. A yellow and far from green enemy was at his devilish defensive best in that green and yellow land. Apart from Llango I never saw a Japanese defensive position that wasn't brilliantly conceived in its use of nature, and fanatically held. On the other hand I never saw a Japanese attack which couldn't have been planned by a competent Boy Scout.

* * *

The Gurkhas and West Yorks were making our initial attempt to deal with 'Pots' and my Company spent its first few days sitting in a defensive rôle round Brigade Headquarters, and patrolling by night. 'Pots' was like a large inverted 'L', its longer base lying across the road and its upright pointing towards Kwa Sipahi, and after three days' fighting we held most of the upright while the Jap positions had been roughly located in the far corners and across the road to the right.

On the night of May 13 a Gurkha Battalion, the 1/10th was to attack right-handed towards the road, and we were to carry on and clear that part of the village which lay on the far side.

Our C.O. took with him 'B' and 'C' Companies with four three-inch mortar detachments and the Pioneer Platoon, and each Company had a troop of tanks and a detachment of Indian Sappers and Miners in support.

Though the fighting was very confused the night attack went well, and at 10.00 hrs the C.O. and I went forward to reconnoitre our part of the show. He had allotted 'B' Company to the right and 'C' Company to the left of a small stream dividing the area to be attacked, and apart from giving zero hour as 13.30 hrs little further planning was possible because as usual there was no indication of the existence of any enemy positions on the far side of the road.

The air war was entirely ours that day, and we watched the Mitchells flying overhead to bomb somewhere up the Tiddim road and the Vultee Vengeances up-ending themselves like ducks on a pond before a screaming dive to drop their bomb cluster on the targets just ahead of us. But in the matter of artillery things had considerably evened up owing to our rationed ammunition supply, and the Japs in addition to their short-range Battalion field gun had brought up 7 mm, 105 mm, and 150 mm guns, and were using them to considerable effect. These two latter types were mostly used for harassing fire and their shells could be heard coming in suffi-

TIDDIM

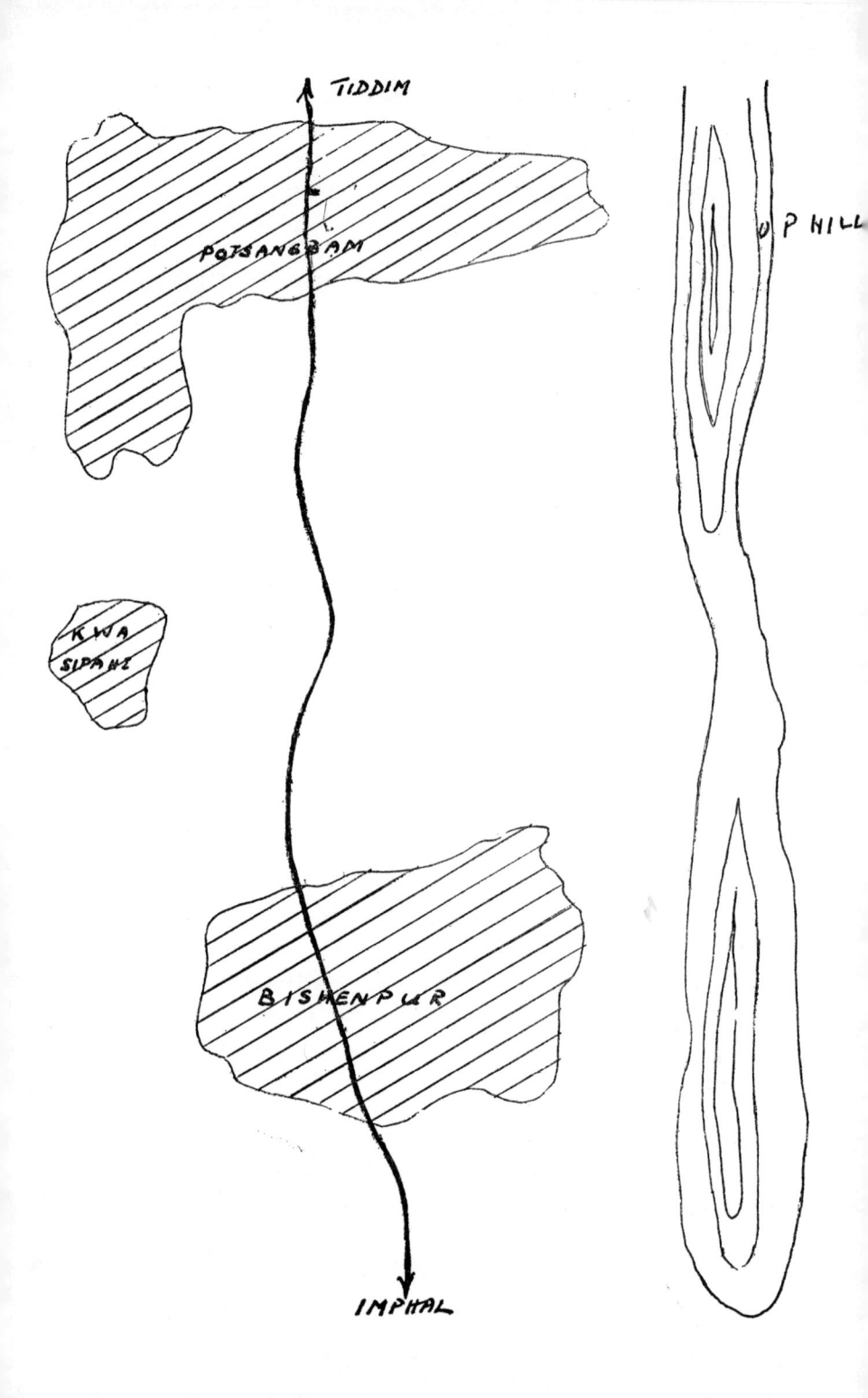

POTSANGBAM

OP HILL

KWA SIPAHI

BISHENPUR

IMPHAL

cient time to get under cover if there happened to be any. But their 75's up in the hills at right-angles to the road had direct observation of all our movements.

Trying to escape some of this shelling while moving up to the attack on 'Pots and Pans' 'B' Company ran into some long-range machine-gun fire from the edge of the wood which was our objective. Several casualties had already been suffered when the Company eventually reached me, and two sections of 10 Platoon were still pinned down in the open paddy field. But it could not be helped, and I gave out orders to Johnty, now acting as Second-in-Command to the Company, to L/Cpl. Brown, the senior N.C.O. left in 10 Platoon, to John Davison—at last we had an officer in command of 11 Platoon —and to Sgt. Larke commanding 12 Platoon, to the mortar detachment commander, to an R.E. officer, to my Company Sergeant-Major, to an officer from the 1/10 Gurkhas who were supporting us, and finally to the 3rd Carabinier Troop Commander who had brought up his three Lee tanks.

The width of our attack needed two Platoons, and I had only two. So there were not many orders to give beyond allotting bounds on which we would halt to ensure control and which we tried to identify from an aerial map which I had 'forgotten' to return to the Brigadier.

There was none of the thrill of a starlight night about our start line this time. The sun blazed hot on the dusty blousy vegetation, so pocked with mortar and grenade marks from the battle of the night before. Trees and bamboo clumps were blacked with fire or splintered by bullets, and a heap of Japanese equipment and weapons lay near and—mute evidence of the price paid to collect them—a tangle of bloody field dressings.

Ahead the vegetation looked thicker and greener, but the bridge across the stream lurched stupidly on its side, and our start line on the road was straddled with Vengeance bomb craters. There was no sign or sound of movement. But 10 Platoon's already depleted ranks proved that the Japs were there all right, and more of us were soon going to be shot at to find out exactly where. In short there were better ways of spending a warm Sunday afternoon in May.

However the mortars were soon crumping down their fire to see us across the road, and a few minutes later we were fifty yards in and both Platoons safely over their first bound. No sooner had 11 Platoon started off again—slightly right-handed this time—than up went the curtain on a show which was to have no interval for the next five hours. In we went on a frontage of less than two hundred yards, and by the end we had penetrated three hundred yards into that beastly wood and the Company which dug in that night was to be less than forty strong.

There are few tactics to describe in that sort of battle and it was like ferreting rabbits which could answer back. 11 Platoon caught it first. They snooped forward, a pair at a time, and the Japs let them come until two Sections had their nearest men within ten yards of the bunkers. Both Bren Gunners, both Section Commanders, and the Platoon Commander were hit at once, and as I reached Platoon Headquarters Sgt. Kelley was waving back the stretcher-bearers and trying to organize covering fire to get at the wounded. We were being sniped from behind now too, and as I turned back from waving a Section to go and deal with it, I saw Sgt. Kelley coming back across the open with John Davison slung across his shoulder. He had pulled him out alive, and had covered thirty yards in the open without being touched himself.

From the bodies in the undergrowth in front if from nothing else we now knew where our first obstacle lay. We knew too how much was clear of mines, and the obvious answer was to get our tanks into action at once. I pressed the bell at the back of the nearest Lee, took out the speaker and headphones, and feeling rather as if ordering a taxi, asked for three minutes' shoot with all they had got against targets we would indicate with tracer.

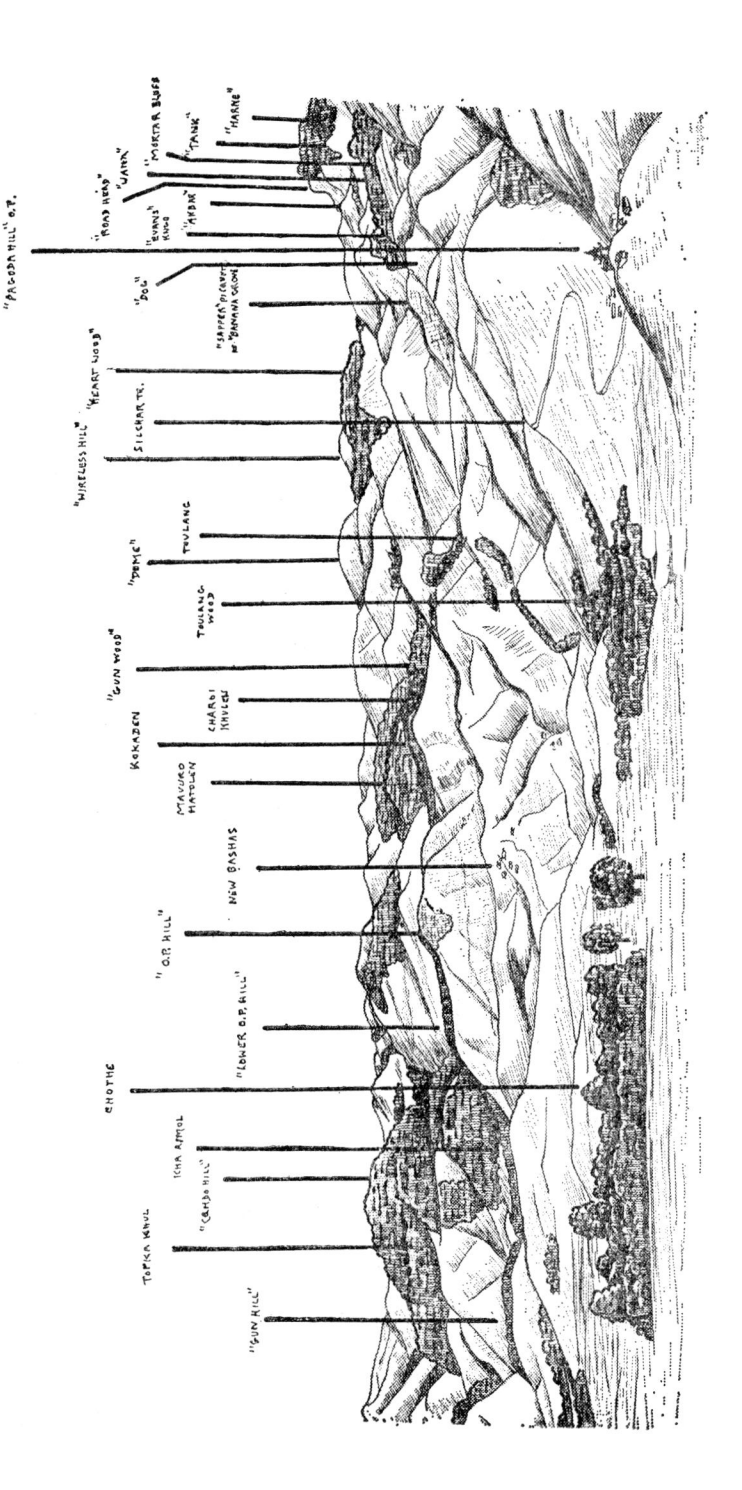

Composite Panorama sketched from Ninthoukhong, Potsangbam, Kwa Sipahi, and Bishenpur.

JAPANESE 47MM A'TK GUN CAPTURED AT POTSANGBAM MAY 15TH 1944.
One of two guns taken by 'C' Coy 9 Border.

Pte. Towner. S.
Int. Sec. 9th Border. 18th Dec. 1944.

Sgt. Larke and I worked round to the right with 12 Platoon to the tune of comforting chatter from two of the tanks' Brownings and 3.7s, and then the tanks started edging forward through the long grass. Of the two runners and the batman who usually formed my links, one had been wounded and the others were away on jobs. Company Commanders had frequently been censured, and rightly too by the C.C. for getting over-involved in a battle, and I suddenly found myself right out of it. The tanks stopped shooting, and next to the smacks of grenades was added an outburst of shouting which held an unmistakable ring. Triumph or terror, British or Japanese, it was the primitive sound which comes when emotions are roused and unchecked. It was obvious that everyone was now at it hand-to-hand.

When I caught up again most of it seemed over. There was a line of nine smallish bunkers beyond the usual brushwood fence, and Sgt. Stratford's Section had swept on and was lining a ditch on the open edge of the village while the rest of the Platoon had gone to ground along the bunker line.

Almost to a man the Japs had died without trying to escape. But one was burning in the open, and his yellow limbs were black and shining like those of some fantastic negro; another who had come out to fight was dead and sprawling, a bayonet like an outsize arrow still sticking in his chest; three more, already wounded, were running for the cover of a tall bamboo clump some thirty yards away.

My first grenade was a wide. My next, though a full pitch, dealt with the nearest of the runners. The second was hit by Stratford's Section covering the rear, and the third reached cover untouched but chased all the way by Rudlin's 2-inch mortar which was now firing, so it seemed, between my legs. But the Platoon had not escaped, and in front of nearly every bunker lay a body which would not move again. Among them was that of Sgt. Larke—whose victory it was.

The next drill was to make sure the bunkers were clear, and as Section Commanders were in short supply I collected the nearest man. He somehow turned out to be Johnty, who had come up to join in the fight.

The first two bunkers were either empty or contained Japs we soon proved to be dead. In front of the third lay Sgt. Larke, his arm outstretched for throwing his last grenade, and as I approached I saw a rifle muzzle move through the slit and I felt the blast of cordite in my face as a bullet whizzed safely by. This was followed from another quarter by a grenade which struck me smartly on the heel but did not explode, and since a sniper's bullet next blew off the tip of my bayonet within an inch of my right eyebrow, I began to feel I was a bit unpopular and I retired like an ostrich behind a slender tree.

Then began one of those stupid, brave displays which made people wonder why the 14th Army took so long to reconquer Burma. That little Jap had no thought but to inflict as many casualties as he could before he fell beside his dead companion in the bunker, and this time we got off fairly lightly—but not before he had killed the two wounded who lay within his narrow range.

The sequence was to drop in a grenade on him and then follow up with a bayonet, but it did not work quite so easily. In spite of my smart backward jump I still seemed to be nearer the forward slit than anyone else—and there was no lack of volunteers to hand me extra grenades. It had to be a left-handed lob, and when my first two burst outside the bunker I thought my aiming was at fault. The third was a dud, but I watched the fourth more carefully and saw it bounce back and realized the little Nip was having time to catch them and throw them back.

Letting the pin of the next one go, I counted up to what seemed like three and three-quarters of its four seconds' life and slipped it down the hole. That was the end, but that one Jap had held us up for nearly half an hour.

So it went on through that hot afternoon. I remember three men in ten minutes shot neatly through the throat by some devilish sniper, one of them a Pioneer who had just brought

JAPANESE LIGHT TANK KNOCKED OUT AT NINTHOUKHONG. MAY 1944.

PTE. TOWNER. S. INF SEC. 9TH BORDER 18TH DEC. 1944.

Jap Bunker Position on North Bank of Nullah in Potsangbam. May 15th 1944.

Pte. Towner J.
Int. Sec. 9th Border 18th Dec. 1944.

up extra ammunition and who died because I told him to wait before returning. I remember wondering where to find one extra man when suddenly there appeared in our midst the rest of 10 Platoon, released from their trap in the open by the course of the battle. I remember the burning Jap whose ammunition caught fire and let off a ghostly volley as we passed him; I remember Sgt. Bussey, blood streaming down his face from a nasty head wound, reporting back to me, 'I've been hit, sir,' and standing to attention as if he had been in Company office.

Fighting a battle affects men in different ways, and I remember one strong unwounded soldier on his knees and unable to move, and yet another crawling forward with the leading Section. He was carrying an empty and useless two-inch mortar, and the bombs had been expended hours before.

For the first time, too, that day I saw two men crack. One, a six-foot corporal, who spent the afternoon cowering in a ditch, the other, a reinforcement who when nothing was happening in the middle of the night suddenly broke and ran—until someone stopped him with a bayonet.

In one place there were mines and the little Indian Sappers came forward to clear them. They did a grand job of work with their steel helmets wobbling on their heads, their feet encased in boots so big that they seemed to follow on long after the feet within them had left the ground.

And with it all, as night fell, just three hundred more yards of Potsangbam was ours. There were six hundred still to go.

* * *

Orders came through to hold what we had gained. Wire and ammunition came up, and we dug in and finished at midnight. Five minutes later firing broke out in all directions. Some shelling and a small Japanese counter-attack in another part of the village had set everything off, and guns, mortars and tanks were all in action. But we lay for two hours without firing a shot, and I for one wasn't sorry because our part of the line was pretty thin. One Platoon was down to nine, another had no N.C.O. and was commanded by a private soldier named Conery who had done grand work all day. Once again I was the only officer left, and Company Headquarters had lost a stretcher-bearer and two runners and was in imminent danger of losing Green, who insisted on lying on all the reserve ammunition.

Soon after daylight our patrols returned to say to my surprise that Potsangbam was now completely clear of the enemy, and I went through myself to the far end. I found nine of our burnt-out tanks and the stench of death in a sunny nullah, the measure of the failure of a previous attack.

What few Japs were left had cleared out, and I knew we must have been on the fringe of victory the night before. But we had paid the price. That morning the Padre buried Johnty —I'd sent him back out of the battle but he had been hit by a stray mortar bomb—Sgt. Larke, Private Ward from Dentdale who could neither read nor write but who had certainly saved my life once that day before he had stopped a sniper's bullet in the fading light, Durkin who died with his Bren gun blazing and, I'm sure, a joke on his lips, Barlow, the absent-minded who could never remember to write to his mother, Watkinson, a fine, quiet soldier, whose baby daughters were now orphaned. These and a dozen others were laid together in a rough grave beside that jungle path.

The clearing of Potsangbam enabled the General to make the final move in the plan aimed at destroying 33 Division. The two other Battalions of our Brigade had already established their road block ten miles further up the road, and 63 Brigade with ourselves still under command were to slice into the hills on the right flank to prevent the Japs from turning back.

After two nights' rest we set off and reached our first objectives by dawn. The situation down the road was now so complicated that it was evident a climax must soon be reached.

Behind us towards Imphal the Japs had twice established temporary road blocks and an impertinent Jap raiding party had attacked Divisional Headquarters and the Administrative Box. In front of them a Brigade from 20 Division was faced by an equivalent number of enemy. We came next in this many-decked and multi-coloured sandwich, with the rest of the Jap 33 Division between us and 48 Brigade's road block.

The air was ours, the road usually ours too, but both sides could supply isolated bodies by means of mule trains going off into the blue of the hills and round the flanks.

For our first move 'B' Company were in reserve, and 'A' Company made a successful attack on a ridge known as O.P. Hill. Next day, however, 'B' Company set off for an isolated action against some Japs reported on a hill beyond.

The monsoon had begun and we had a wet start. We had no groundsheets and no spare clothing, and before we set off the Sergeant-Major threatened to put a man on a charge for washing in the water in which he had slept.

One battle is much like another to those who fight them, and suffice it to say that there was the usual unexpected nullah en route, the usual surprises when all went well, the usual reactions when things went badly, the usual bullets to kick up the dust at our feet or whine overhead, the usual strong Company of Japs where rumour had placed the usual underfed Section ready to surrender on account of the usual ammunition shortage.

We took the first part of the hill easily and then ran into some nasty sniping with explosive bullets. After a frantic hour trying to correct the artillery searching for a target—when 'pluses' fell out of sight into a nullah beyond and any 'minuses' hit us in the back of the neck—we attacked again and took the top of the hill. It was then too late and too dark to hold it.

Recalled to the Battalion some four miles back towards the plains, we found others sleeping in our water holes. Wearily we redug, and we settled down for two hours' sleep. Some more good blood had been spilt, a few more Japs would snipe no more. Another day was past, and its jokes and sunshine would be remembered long after its dangers and discomforts.

Just one more day nearer the end.

The grave of Capt. R. L. Hetherington five yards from the spot where he died in action Feb. 6th 1944.

XIII

UP THE CHIMNEY

'A' Company was sent in to do the same job the day after 'B' Company's not too successful attack, and Green and I, escorted by a Platoon of 'D' Company, climbed back up O.P. Hill to tell Mike Hodgson in command of 'A' Company all we had learned about the Japs the day before. Thus I spent most of the morning talking while the guns and mortars were ranging, and after quite a sizeable barrage the attack started at midday.

The Japs proved no less stubborn than the previous day, and their strength on the reverse slopes caused the attack to be called off at 18.00 hrs. Two further hours passed before the wounded had been cleared away and 'A' Company was back on O.P. Hill.

At midnight Mike and I lay down to sleep in a bunker. An hour or two later we were awakened by high-pitched Japanese voices, and next came the unpleasant realization that the enemy had over-run the forward point of our perimeter. From the noise and the showers of grenades bursting round us the Nips were barely twenty yards away. This was much too close to our way of thinking, and we collected the C.S.M. and two men from the nearest bunker and started throwing things at them to show our displeasure.

Mike fired off the S.O.S. signal with his Verey pistol, and this brought immediate response from the guns on the plains below—a response which may have caused some shells to land on 33 Division H.Q. but had no noticeable effect on our attackers. The 3-inch mortars with which I did a little private shoot proved no more successful and only seemed to sting two new lots of Japs on our flank into action.

From the sound of their shooting it appeared they already possessed some of our Bren guns, or perhaps had just captured them. Mike now left me and went back to organize troops for a counter-attack, and the next hour, punctuated by grunts and bangs and digging noises as the Japs worked hard to consolidate what they had won, passed somewhat murkily.

Mike did not return—I learned later he had been killed by a burst which hit him in the throat—and I started to stroll back over the hill to get reinforcements for our front perimeter. There were so many grenades going off all round me that it was like walking on beech nuts. But they were made in Japan and seemed comparatively harmless, until suddenly something like the kick of a mule exploded in my leg. What my mother has since proudly called an 'expensive' bullet had taken a short cut through my right thigh, and I subsided gently backwards into a slit trench. And thus ignominiously and with my back to the enemy, ended my personal fight with Japan.

Like the rest of the wounded, I had to evacuate myself by my own efforts because we could not afford a man away from the perimeter. So, a bit bemused and filled with the idea of keeping my leg in the air, I set off head first down the side of a steep khud amid a small avalanche of stones and bits of jungle. Landing before long on the path below, I was caught by a gunner and his Sikh signaller who were also on their way out. They took my rifle off my back and slung it between them, and with my elbows over butt and muzzle they dragged me another mile and left me beside a stream as dawn was breaking. There I was picked up by some of our own stretcher-bearers, and reached our Regimental Aid Post about 07.00 hrs.

The M.O. tried to send me to sleep while the Brigadier tried to keep me awake, and in the end I went back in a jeep to the Advanced Dressing Station at Bishenpur to wait for an ambulance. But the Advanced Dressing Station promptly got itself surrounded by Japs, and with some twenty equally battered soldiers I spent the night in a tent, waking occasionally to hear the odd bullet pinging through the canvas.

The road was cleared by about 18.00 hrs next evening and the first ambulance through got blown up. Fortunately I was in the second one, and I arrived in fair condition at the hospital in Imphal.

Next morning I was shovelled into a Dakota. By mistake it nearly took Green too, and I was flown out of Burma up that same chimney down which all our food and ammunition had come over Jap heads for so many weeks.

14th Army badge

This badge was designed by General Sir William Slim himself: the shield represented the defence of India; the sword pointed down rather than up, as is usual practice, to denote the reconquest of Burma from north to south; the hilt of the sword read '14' in Morse code; the cross-piece was S-shaped to represent Slim; and the whole shield was red and black, these being the 14th Army's colours.

EPILOGUE

The 'B' Company I knew was not reconstituted after I left it. Out of a strength of ninety it suffered twenty-two casualties in the attack on O.P. Hill the day before I was wounded, and during the following night 'D' Company lost even more. So 'B' and 'D' Companies were merged together and they did not separate again till the Battalion, back in India, was reinforced for the main drive to Rangoon. But for more reasons than one that final phase must make another story. I merely know that after all their patient slogging in the hills our faithful mules were discarded for 3-tonners, and that our jeeps were changed for Sherman tanks.

It thus became an easier war, and one of swift decisive moves which caught the enemy in the open or on the run, and in the first five months of 1945 it carried the Battalion eight hundred miles from Kalewa to Rangoon. Apart from the vast problem of air supply it also became an easier war to comprehend. After one brief action near Meiktila, for instance, the new 'B' Company counted ninety-two Jap dead—a different story from our weeks of hammering at the bunkers of the Chin Hills, or the single corpse acclaimed a triumph after long hours of waiting beside an ambush in the depths of the tangled jungle.

Many of the old 'B' Company fought on and saw the end, in fact thirty-one of them were there when the last draft sailed for home and the 9th Battalion was no more. But since that night on O.P. Hill they had been scattered throughout the

Edge of airstrip NSUKINA —
Sherman tanks, Airfield-const equip, & Casualty evac plane

NSUKTUA, April 29, 1945
S/sgt Tec
147 JSC 1st Bomber Comd

Meiktila Mar 14 1945
S. Turner, Pte
Int Sec, The Border Regt.
14
Bn Cemetery Meiktila — those killed on
March 2nd in initial attack

reorganized Battalion, and even Dade and Green of my old Company H.Q. now found themselves ranged on the side of authority as members of the C.O.'s orderly room staff. Yet, if I cannot tell of the romance of the road to Mandalay or of how the Fourteenth Army raced the monsoon to the sea, I am certain that the little things would still have remained the real things.

When I started to write this small book I could still have told you of the phases of the Burma moon or of how long it took the morning mists to rise from the floor of the valley. And if I could not always remember the exact day of the week I still knew the feel of a scabbard against my side. In a hospital bed it was a never-ending delight to be able to move one's toes untramelled by a boot, and the easy way the light switched on or water ran from the taps continued to please and surprise me for a long time. Perhaps the reason why the old soldier is reputed to dramatize his story is because he cannot create for those who do not know 'the tiny stuffless voices of the dark', nor can he fully explain the change in the vital values of the ordinary things of life. The contrast is too great, and to my mind every returning soldier should be given time to re-tune his mind. How else can he become used to the blessed certainty of daily bread, or view the setting sun without a twinge of fear?

*   *   *

On leaving Imphal I was flown into another world. Those hospital days were a purgatory between the old life and the new. No place of suffering, but a period of waiting and a time of rest from making decisions. Those constant and fateful decisions of war were behind me, the everyday responsibilities of family life were yet to come.

Now, back among the fells of Westmorland where my story started, my children live because men no different from myself have died. Johnty has a daughter he will not see, and each time I travel up the dale I stop to speak to one of Charles Ward's family, to a wife, whose words of hopeful waiting I had had to read to her soldier husband, and five children illiterate like their father who 'did not really hold with education' but who, like him, are full of the wisdom that does not come from books. My friends Dade and Precious live as if they had never been away from home. I have waited (but not as attentively as he would have done) on Arthur Green at his simple wedding and yet Taffy Young and Rocky Knight and Little and Sergeant Larke had to die.

How much greater than the whole is the individual story of each man, and how much more tragic or joyful is each human thread than the huge pattern in which it plays its tiny part.

Whatever History may write, the lasting memory is Man. The living, loving, hating, thinking soul, his is the story in whatever company it may be set. . . .